Operation Title

Operation Title

Sink the Tirpitz

Glyn L. Evans

Pen & Sword
MARITIME

First published in Great Britain in 2024 by
Pen & Sword Military
An imprint of
Pen & Sword Books Ltd
Yorkshire - Philadelphia

ISBN 978 1 39905 019 7

Typeset in INDIA by IMPEC eSolutions
Printed and bound in England by CPI (UK) Ltd.

Pen & Sword Books Ltd. incorporates the Imprints of Pen & Sword Archaeology,
Atlas, Aviation, Battleground, Discovery, Family History, History, Maritime,
Military, Naval, Politics, Railways, Select, Transport, True Crime, Fiction,
Frontline Books, Leo Cooper, Praetorian Press, Seaforth Publishing,
Wharncliffe and White Owl.

For a complete list of Pen & Sword titles please contact

PEN & SWORD BOOKS LIMITED
47 Church Street, Barnsley, South Yorkshire, S70 2AS, England
E-mail: enquiries@pen-and-sword.co.uk
Website: www.pen-and-sword.co.uk

or

PEN AND SWORD BOOKS
1950 Lawrence Rd, Havertown, PA 19083, USA
E-mail: uspen-and-sword@casematepublishers.com
Website: www.penandswordbooks.com

This book is dedicated to the memory of Able Seaman Robert Paul Evans RN, D/JX 283626, and to all those who, undertaking similar dangerous and hazardous missions, shared his fate.

Contents

Foreword

Courage comes in many forms; history is shaped in many ways. In this fascinating story of one Second World War operation, on the fringes of the main areas of action between the remoteness of the Shetland Islands and isolated Norwegian fjords, Glyn Evans leaves the courage implicit and the historical focus on one very junior member of the armed forces. Both are unusual presentations, but they work.

Operation Title was an attack against what Churchill called 'The Beast', the German battleship, *Tirpitz*, sister ship to the well-known *Bismarck* that was sunk by British naval forces in May 1941. By October 1942, *Tirpitz* was hiding in a Norwegian fjord, its very presence there a threat to the Arctic and Atlantic convoys, epitomized by the disaster that was Convoy PQ17. Something had to be done, and as aerial assault by the RAF had tried and failed, that something had to be something different. The key was provided by the attack by Italian frogmen riding a *maiale*, basically a torpedo with seats, against the British battleships *Valiant* and *Queen Elizabeth* in Alexandria harbour in December 1941.

What evolved was the joint British-Norwegian Operation Title, involving British frogmen riding 'chariots', again basically torpedoes with seats, being taken from the Shetland Islands to their target, the *Tirpitz*, in its Norwegian fjord, by Norwegians in a small fishing vessel. In relating the story and describing the boat, men and machines involved, Glyn Evans draws heavily on official records. The moral, emotional and physical courage of those involved is understated by these documents, and Glyn Evans' purposeful avoidance of comment leaves that courage chillingly implicit. The focus, however, is on just one member of the British frogman team: the junior member, Able Seaman Robert Paul Evans (no relation, although one gets a feeling that Glyn Evans regrets this). The operation goes wrong, and both Norwegians and British make their escapes to Sweden. But along the way there is a fire-fight, Evans is wounded, and he cannot make his escape. In relating what then happened to Able Seaman Evans, the author exposes the criminality of the Nazi war machine.

Earlier books, often by participants, have related the story and heroics of 'The Shetland Bus', but they were written from the usual historical context of those in command. This book, with its simplicity of focus on just one of The Shetland Bus operations and a small one in the context of a world war and one of its participants, brings home the intimacy of ordinary men doing extraordinary things, making it an important adjunct to that litany.

Dr David J. Parry, MA, PhD (retired Royal Navy submarine commanding officer and author of *Perisher*, the story of the RN submarine commanding officers' qualifying course)

Introduction

'His ashes in a peaceful urn shall rest,
His name a great example stands to show
How strangely high endeavours may be blessed
Where piety and valour jointly go.'

When one hears one's name mentioned in conversation across a crowded room, one's ear immediately picks up on it. In the same way, when reading printed matter, one's own name tends to leap out from the page. So it happened that, when reading the book *Max Horton and the Western Approaches*, I readily spotted my surname, Evans, on page 136: 'the whole party went ashore, making for the Swedish frontier. All got across safely except Able Seaman Evans, who was wounded in a brush with a German patrol.'

This biography of Admiral Sir Max Kennedy Horton, GCB DSO, recounts, *inter alia*, his submarine service in the First World War, his command of the reserve fleet between the wars, being Vice Admiral [Submarines] (HMS *Dolphin*) in 1941, and his command of the Western Approaches, Liverpool, from November 1942. After some research, I discovered that the Evans in question no relation of mine was Able Seaman Robert Paul Evans RN, and my book, *Operation Title*, tells the story of how a lowly able seaman came to warrant a mention in a book about an admiral.

Robert Paul 'Bob' Evans was born in Camberwell, London, in 1922. Seventeen years later, we find him living at Maiden Erlegh Stud Farm, Beech Lane, Wokingham, Berkshire. How he came to be there in 1939 is a matter of conjecture, but my theory is that, as Bob came from the Camberwell/Brixton part of London, he was given a job there thanks to the philanthropy of 'Solly' Joel [see Notes].

We catch up with Evans two years later, on 18 June 1941, when he reported to HMS *St Vincent* to offer his service to the Fleet Air Arm; he was 19 years old and would, in any event, have received a formal call-up on his twentieth birthday. He was given his service number, FX 88794, and rated N.A. 2, naval aircraftsman second class Period of Service 'Until the end of the present emergency'. Details on his record sheet show his occupation at that time as 'Traveller', which was a common term found on many registration papers of the day, the current equivalent possibly being sales representative. His height was recorded as 6ft 1⅜in, his chest 38½in, hair 'fair', eyes 'hazel blue' and complexion 'fresh'. Having completed these formalities, he was immediately released to the reserve list to await his call-up. This came on 26 September 1941, when Evans was attached to HMS *Daedalus* and given a new service number, D/JX 283626, his Royal Navy number, the 'D' denoting Devonport. Via time in HMS *St Vincent*, HMS *Drake* and HMS *Raleigh*, Evans found himself in HMS *Dolphin* – home of the Royal Navy Submarine Service – on 20 April 1942 and was, two months later, in what was to be his final posting, HMS *Titania*. Details of these various ships and shore establishments can be found in the Notes section at the end of this book. It is more than likely that Evans' transfer to *Dolphin* was a result of him having responded to the notice, posted by Commanders Sladen and Fell in all RN barracks, seeking volunteers for 'dangerous and hazardous missions'.

Integral to the story of Operation Title, the Allied mission in October 1942 to sink the German battleship *Tirpitz*, is an account of the Italian Navy's raid on Alexandria harbour in December 1941, the ill-fated Arctic Convoy PQ17 – which set sail for Russia on 27 June 1942 – the allied commando raid on Sark (Operation Basalt) in October 1942, and the Royal Engineers' glider-borne mission to Norway (Operation Freshman) in November 1942. Also recorded here is the devastating effect of Hitler's infamous secret 'Commando Order' of 18 October 1942.

Prime Minister Winston Churchill referred to *Tirpitz* as 'The Beast', and on 25 January 1942, he wrote: 'The destruction or even the crippling of this ship is the greatest event at this present time. No other target is comparable to it.' Between January and April 1942, in five unsuccessful attempts to sink *Tirpitz*, the RAF lost fifteen aircraft and ninety-seven RAF crew. Churchill's words, however, had sown the seeds for Operation Title. Harvesting began on 26 October 1942, when the 55ft wooden fishing boat *Arthur* [see Notes 2] sailed from Scalloway, Shetland, with a crew of four Norwegians, a six-man team of Royal Navy divers and two 'chariots', in a brave attempt to tame 'The Beast'.

For the sake of authenticity, and where they exist, this story is told through contemporary reports of events by the men involved. The stark realities revealed by these reports render other words superfluous.

The verse that heads up this 'Introduction' comes from *Heroic Stanzas on the Death of Oliver Cromwell*, written in 1658 by John Dryden. Later in the book, the relevance of the last two lines will become clear.

Glyn L. Evans
('Cambria', Kent, December 2022)

Chapter 1

The Threat

With just three survivors from a complement of 1,418 officers and men, HMS *Hood* (the 'Mighty Hood'), a Royal Navy battle-cruiser of 46,602 tonnes, fell victim to the pride of Hitler's navy, the German battleship *Bismarck*, on 24 May 1941. After a cat-and-mouse chase and a battle royal, *Bismarck* was itself sunk three days later, but not before giving the Allies a reminder of just how big a threat was posed by a ship of its class. Into that same class fell its sister ship, *Tirpitz*.

Tirpitz was indeed a 'Beast' – the name given to it by Winston Churchill – as its vital statistics show:

Length   817ft overall, 792ft at the waterline
Breadth   118ft
Draft   33.75ft
Armament
8 x 15in guns in twin turrets; range 41,500 yards (23.5 miles)
12 x 5.9in guns in twin turrets; range 27,000 yards (15.3 miles)
16 x 4.1in twin anti-aircraft guns
40 smaller AA guns
2 x triple 21in torpedo tubes

4 x Scout seaplanes via two athwartships catapults
Armour plating   main 13in, upper 5.7in
Design Speed   30.25 knots
Complement   103 officers, 1,962 men

Prior to those words of Churchill, the RAF had launched six sorties against *Tirpitz* between October 1940 and June 1941, without success and at the cost of four aircraft. Taking up on Churchill's words, the RAF launched a further five attacks, the last on 28/29 April 1942, resulting in the loss overall of another fifteen aircraft and almost one hundred aircrew with no discernible result. Some other method would need to be devised. As had been proved with *Bismarck*, a full naval engagement against *Tirpitz* would be costly, while its mere existence, in that area of the North Sea off the coast of German-occupied Norway, was tying up a large number of Allied ships that could more usefully be deployed elsewhere.

There is no doubt the most devastating effect of the *Tirpitz* threat manifested itself in the decimation of the Allied Arctic Convoy PQ17, a collection of thirty-five merchant ships with attendant escort vessels which sailed from Reykjavik, Iceland, for Russia on 27 June 1942, under Convoy Commander Captain J.C.K. Dowding, DSO RD RNR. Also at sea, under the command of Admiral Tovey, was a battleship covering force, within steaming distance of PQ17 should it become apparent that the German big ships were to be deployed. Two merchant ships had to return shortly after leaving port, while the remainder of the convoy steamed on for Archangel in northern Russia, carrying vital war supplies. At 5.00 am on 4 July, the attack on the convoy began with a single He 115 diving through cloud to release a torpedo which hit the US freighter, *Christopher Newport*. Damaged to such an extent it had to be abandoned, its crew was picked up by two of the three dedicated rescue ships attached to the convoy. Shortly after, the vessel's sinking was hastened by a torpedo from the RN submarine P-614.

At 7.30 pm, a force of Ju 88s and He 115 torpedo aircraft attacked but were beaten off by the aggressive tactics of the US destroyer *Wainwright*, sailing towards the low-flying Heinkels with all guns blazing. No torpedo hits were scored, and the bombers likewise met with no success. However, a more serious attack developed at 8.20 pm when a force of around thirty He 111s released their torpedoes right in the middle of the convoy. Four aircraft were shot down, but torpedo hits were scored on three ships. The *Navarino* settled and sank, while the *William Hooper* had to be abandoned and was later finished off by a U-boat's torpedo. The Russian tanker *Azerbaijan*, although hit just forward of the engine room, was able to continue steaming while a fire on board caused by the explosion was successfully extinguished by its crew.

It had been with considerable misgivings that the Admiralty agreed to the sailing of PQ17. The German occupation of Norway, which began on 9 April 1940, had given the Nazis deep, naturally well-protected anchorages for their warships and access to airfields for bombers and torpedo aircraft, all with easy access to the North Sea routes of the Arctic convoys. During the time between the Norwegian occupation and June 1942, German forces had ample opportunity to reinforce these advantages. Thus, from a naval point of view, PQ17 was a most unsound operation of war, but political considerations were paramount. The Russians were fighting desperately to stem the German advance towards Moscow, and American ships, loaded with war materials of all kinds, were arriving daily in Iceland for onward transit to northern Russian ports. British and American transport experts favoured the longer but safer route into Russia via the Persian Gulf, but Stalin, failing to understand or ignoring the difficulties to be overcome, dictated that aid should be sent via the shorter, northerly route. Both Churchill and Roosevelt accepted his decision. On 4 July, even as the escort vessels of PQ17 were resisting with some success the heavy air attacks to which the convoy was being subjected, the First Sea Lord, Admiral Sir Dudley Pound in his London office some 1,800 miles away was conferring with officers from the Naval Intelligence Division regarding the possible location of the German surface ships in general, and *Tirpitz* in particular, relative to this convoy.

For Admiral Pound to make a firm decision on the best option for the further movement of PQ17 he required accurate and up-to-date information on the whereabouts of *Tirpitz*. Naval Intelligence, however, could only state they were 'tolerably certain' that the Narvik force had moved north to Altenfjord, by the North Cape, and that the *Tirpitz* force had joined it there. From Admiral Pound's chart showing the estimated position of PQ17 (and homeward-bound Convoy QP13 nearby, on the opposite course), it was evident that, if the German ships were about to leave or had left Altenfjord, they could intercept either convoy at around 2.00 am on 5 July, just four hours after the last air attack. The possibility was discussed of turning PQ17 back and ordering Admiral Tovey, with his battleship covering force, to steam towards the *Tirpitz* force at high speed. However, this would not have given Stalin the promised supplies and there was the possibility that the merchant ships might not have sufficient fuel to make the return voyage to Iceland. Another possibility was for Admiral Tovey's force to catch up with the convoy and accompany it through to Archangel but, with the fleet's air cover being insufficient to match that which the Germans could put up from their Norwegian land bases, this was not a viable option. Had Tovey's battleships been damaged, then the door to the Atlantic would have been wide open for *Tirpitz* to escape and ultimately inflict far heavier losses on merchant shipping than if the whole of PQ17 were destroyed. A third suggestion was also considered, to withdraw the convoy's close cruiser support and allow PQ17 to continue on its course, keeping only its destroyer escort. While this would keep the merchant ships concentrated for mutual protection against air and U-boat attack, it would make the task of the *Tirpitz* force so much easier that, if they did the job properly, not a single ship would survive.

Having weighed up all the options, Dudley Pound issued three signal orders in quick succession. The first read: 'Cruisers to withdraw to westward at high speed and the convoy to disperse.' The second read: 'Owing to the threat from surface ships convoy is to disperse and proceed to Russian ports.' The third, sent just twenty-three minutes later, added, 'Convoy is to scatter.' That final order has been discussed countless times since and continues to be the subject of fierce debate. The consequences have been covered in great detail elsewhere by maritime historians, so suffice to record here that, of the thirty-five ships of the original convoy, two had turned back, eight had already been sunk by air attack, nine more by U-boats, and seven, which had been damaged by air attack and abandoned, were subsequently sent to the bottom by U-boats. The Germans had achieved all this for the loss of only five aircraft. *Tirpitz* had not fired one shot; its threat had been sufficient.

Chapter 2

A Wake-up Call

The gradual erosion of Britain's naval supremacy on the high seas was gathering pace towards the end of 1941 with the loss of the battleship HMS *Prince of Wales* and the battle-cruiser HMS *Repulse*, both victims of Japanese aerial attacks in the South China Sea on 10 December 1941. For Admiral A.B. Cunningham [see Notes], Commander-in-Chief of the Royal Navy ships in the Mediterranean, the erosion of his fleet had begun one month earlier. Cunningham's main responsibility was for the safety of the convoys heading for Egypt and for Malta, a strategic naval base for the conduct of the war in North Africa. The admiral believed that the main threat to British sea power in the Mediterranean would come from the Italian Fleet; Italy, under Mussolini, having declared war on France and Great Britain on 10 June 1940. Ultimately, this proved to be the case, but not before the Germans, with their extensive fleet of U-boats in those waters, had also made their presence felt.

The aircraft carrier HMS *Ark Royal*, built at Birkenhead by Cammell Laird & Company, was commissioned into the Royal Navy on 16 December 1938. It was involved in the first aerial U-boat kills of the Second World War, operations off Norway, the search for *Bismarck* and in support of the Malta convoys. Surviving several near misses, it gained the reputation as a 'lucky ship' until, on 13 November 1941, a torpedo from the German

U-81 struck, causing *Ark Royal* to sink the following day in 3,300ft of water, 30 miles off Gibraltar.

At 26 years old, the Queen Elizabeth-class battleship HMS *Barham* had seen action at the Battle of Jutland during the First World War and was now part of the Mediterranean Fleet covering Malta convoys. *Barham* had helped in the sinking of an Italian heavy cruiser and a destroyer during the Battle of Cape Matapan (27–29 March 1941) off the southwest coast of the Greek Peloponnese and assisted in the evacuation of Allied troops from Crete. Off the Egyptian coast on 25 November 1941, *Barham* fell victim to a torpedo from the German U-331. As it turned on its side and began sinking fast, a huge explosion tore the ship apart; 862 members of the crew perished.

With these two large losses in such a short space of time serving as a wake-up call, Admiral Cunningham was taking no chances with his two remaining capital ships, HMS *Queen Elizabeth* and HMS *Valiant*, moored in Alexandria harbour. He had earlier warned London that he was worried about losing any more of his main assets: 'I must keep them rather in cotton wool as it won't do to get another put out of action.' The defences at Alexandria were formidable, and British forces there were on high alert. Minefields, detector cables, observer positions and anti-submarine nets protected the port in layers to a considerable distance out to sea. Motorboats cruised within the harbour itself and in the waters off the harbour entrance, while a patrol of destroyers kept watch in the near-distant approaches. The British thus felt they had done everything they could to protect the ships.

After much experimentation involving the use of explosive-packed, high-speed boats driven by almost silent electric motors, the ingenuity and fertile imagination of the Italian Navy came to the fore with the development of an underwater vessel similar to a standard torpedo. This was driven by compressed air and manned by two men, with their heads just above the water's surface, sitting astride it to guide it on its way. Having only a short range, it would be taken on board one of the Royal Italian Navy's fast motorboats and put into the water within striking distance of its selected target. Early success came towards the end of the First World War when, on 31 October 1918, Lieutenants Rossetti and Paolucci took their 'mignata' (leech) into Pola harbour on the Istrian peninsula (now Croatia) and successfully fixed its explosive charge to the 20,000-tonne Austro-Hungarian dreadnought battleship *Viribus Unitis*, which blew up and sank.

Subsequent to this success, the Italian Navy continued the development of these craft, forming their own special naval assault unit. The physical fitness and fortitude of the men involved made for a formidable fighting force, while the Italian flair for design and engineering enabled them to hone their submersible manned torpedo into a weapon of war to be feared. Alongside this development was the need to develop a means by which the men might remain submerged and invisible, enabling them to reach their target undetected. How fortunate, then, were the Italians when the specialist British diving equipment firm of Siebe, Gorman & Company opened an operation in Italy between the world wars. This company produced the Davis Submerged Escape Apparatus (DSEA), an early type of oxygen rebreather invented in 1910 by Sir Robert Davis, the head of the company, which was adopted by the Royal Navy after further development by Davis in 1927. While intended primarily as an emergency escape apparatus for submarine crew, it was soon being used for diving, providing a handy shallow-water diving apparatus giving the user, at that time, a thirty-minute endurance.

The Italian Navy divers gave the submersible torpedo the nickname '*maiale*', which translates into English as 'pig', succinctly summing up its sometimes unpredictable handling characteristics. The *maiale* looked like an ordinary 21in torpedo but with a superstructure added to protect the two pilots. At the front of the 24ft-long hull was the round nose of the warhead containing 660lb of explosive, while behind the warhead and to prevent him being swept off by its speed through the water (3 knots) the pilot had the protection of a small screen which housed a rudimentary instrument panel. Control of the *maiale* was by use of a joystick with a wheel at the end, enabling the pilot to turn left or right. Forward or backward movement of the stick operated the hydroplanes to dive or surface, while on either side were two valves which operated the fore and aft trimming tanks, serving to balance the machine. The main ballast tank was housed behind the forward pilot, and behind that sat the second pilot, holding on to a bar. The latter's job was to cut through any submarine defence nets, remove the warhead and suspend it beneath the target hull. On the conical rear section was the bosun's locker, where the cutting equipment, spare breathing set, rope, clamps and limpet mines were stored. The watertight hull contained the bank of batteries, electric motor, and electrically driven air pumps.

Two months after Italy's declaration of war against Britain, the Italian 10th Flotilla of the Regia Marina began an aggressive search for the Royal Navy, not with the intention of an open battle for which they were ill-equipped, but to strike the British where they were most vulnerable, at times and places where it was least expected. After several failures, which served as both experience and incentive, success came with an attack on shipping in the Gibraltar Roads on 20 September 1941. Having been unable to penetrate the harbour defences of Gibraltar to attack the naval shipping there (HMS *Nelson* and HMS *Ark Royal*), three teams of the 10th Flotilla set their sights on several laden merchant ships anchored offshore. One explosion ripped apart the 2,444-grt (Gross Registered Tonnage) oil depot ship *Fiona Shell*, a second broke the back of the 8,142-grt RFA (Royal Fleet Auxiliary) oiler *Denbydale* and the third put the 10,893-grt tanker *Durham* on the rocks. While the loss of fuel and tonnage was not great, *Durham* later being refloated and towed to Falmouth in Cornwall for repair, the ramifications of the means by which these losses had occurred were serious, to say the least.

If the Admiralty had any doubts as to the cause of these losses, they had only to read the item put out shortly afterwards by the Italian Propaganda Ministry (going totally against the need for operational security) which read: 'Assault craft of the Navy have succeeded in penetrating the Roads and Grand Harbour of Gibraltar where they sank a 10,000-tonne tanker and a 6,000-tonne merchant ship loaded with munitions. A 12,000-tonne merchant ship loaded with war material was hurled against a rocky outcrop by the force of the explosions and can be regarded as lost.' Further evidence of the cause was reported by Vice Admiral Sir James Somerville, commander of force H, a British naval force established to replace French naval power in the western Mediterranean, lost with the signing of the French armistice with Nazi Germany in 1940. Somerville wrote: 'A breathing apparatus, picked up in the commercial anchorage where an oil hulk, the *Fiona Shell*, had been sunk, and ss *Durham* damaged, indicated that the probable cause was attack by two-man submarines.'

Security at Alexandria harbour, by now on high alert, shot itself in the foot on 19 December 1941. Opening the harbour defence chain with its hanging steel mesh to allow access for three British destroyers returning from operations against the Italians in the Gulf of Sirte provided the means by which three Italian *maiale* were able to slip in undetected. Their journey had begun sixteen days before and 1,600 nautical miles away at La Spezia, the home base of the Italian 10th Flotilla, from where they travelled to Leros in three specially built tubes welded to the deck of the submarine *Scirè*. At Leros, the Italian frogmen, who had travelled there separately and under the utmost secrecy, boarded *Scirè* for onward transit south to a position about a mile off Alexandria. Here, the *maiale* were released from their pens on the deck of the submerged submarine and mounted by their riders. Once inside the harbour, the three *maiale* split up and headed for their respective targets: Lieutenant de la Penne for the battleship HMS *Valiant*, Captain Marceglia for the battleship HMS *Queen Elizabeth* and Captain Martellotta for the aircraft carrier HMS *Illustrious*. As it had not been confirmed for certain that the latter was in harbour – and it proved not to be – Martellotta's instructions were to attack any of the large oil tankers known to be there. The *maiale* had not reached the peak of perfection, but were nevertheless operationally effective, so despite their struggles, each crew was able to place its charges exactly as planned. Suffice to say that the operation was a complete success, ending one of the most imaginative and daring raids of the war to date. While all six Italian frogmen found themselves prisoners of war, they had completed their mission with courage and audacity, giving the Royal Navy both food for thought and a bloody nose from which it would take some time to recover. *Queen Elizabeth* and *Valiant* would be out of action for some considerable time.

Chapter 3

Playing Catch-up

'David took up five small stones from the stream and put them in his bag. With his catapult ready, he went out to meet Goliath.' (1 Samuel 17, v 40)

The Admiralty's initial response to the Italian raid at Alexandria was to look for ways to improve the harbour defences, and it was to be some while before thoughts turned from defence to attack. The catalyst for a change of mindset came in the form of the following memorandum from Churchill to Major-General Hastings Ismay for the Chiefs of Staff Committee, sent on 18 January 1942:

'Please report what is being done to emulate the exploits of the Italians in Alexandria Harbour and similar methods of this kind. At the beginning of the War a number of bright ideas on this subject received very little encouragement. Is there any reason why we should be incapable of the same kind of scientific aggressive action that the Italians have shown? One would have thought we should be in the lead. Please state the exact position.'

How times had changed: in their book *Above us the Waves*, co-authors C.E.T. Warren and James Benson point out that it was before and during the First World War that proposals for a human torpedo were turned down by the First Lord of the Admiralty, a post held at that time by the Liberal Member of Parliament for Dundee, the Rt Hon. Winston Churchill.

The 'scientific aggressive action' called for by Churchill in his memorandum became the responsibility of the Royal Navy's vice admiral (submarines), Admiral Sir Max K. Horton, an experienced and highly respected veteran of the submarine service who had seen action as a submarine commanding officer during the First World War. By the time of his appointment to the post on 9 January 1940, Horton had been mentioned in despatches twice and been awarded the DSO with two bars, the CB (Military) and the KCB. These awards were in addition to others from the grateful governments of Russia, France, Greece and the Netherlands, together with the British Board of Trade Silver Medal for Saving Life at Sea. Horton's aggressive approach was never in doubt and was to manifest itself in his later appointment as Commander-in-Chief Western Approaches, Liverpool, on 17 November 1942, where he masterminded the war against the U-boat menace in what was to become known as the Battle of the Atlantic. As for his scientific qualification, Horton had a stronger grasp than most commanding officers of their boat's mechanical and electrical functions, to the extent that those who should have known more than he of such things, but did not, would often find themselves posted elsewhere.

So began the playing of catch-up. The enormity of the task before Admiral Horton, to build the equivalent of the Italian 'pig' from scratch and to recruit and train the men to use them, required delegation to others at the top of their game and with the necessary experience. Thus, came about the appointment by Horton of two Commanders, W.R. 'Tiny' Fell, DSC, and G.M. 'Slash' Sladen, DSO and DSC. Two better men for the task in hand could not have been chosen. The former, described as 'a sympathetic man of immense charm', had been in the submarine service for twenty-three years. At the beginning of the war, Fell had been appointed commanding officer of submarine *H-43*, hunting U-boats in the Irish Sea. Sladen, described as 'an extraordinarily charismatic man with unlimited energy', had played rugby for England on three occasions and had been a successful submarine commanding officer during the early part of the Second World War. In February 1942, while in command of HM Submarine *Trident*, Sladen torpedoed the German heavy cruiser *Prinz Eugen* off the coast of Norway, severely damaging its stern and causing it to return to Germany for extensive repairs. Both men had survived the notorious Perisher Course.

Perisher is the Royal Navy's Submarine Command Course that a Royal Navy officer must pass before he can be appointed commanding officer of a submarine. The Perisher Course began in 1917 and went on to serve the Royal Navy for 100 years as the backbone of a submarine service that has produced thirteen VCs and countless other awards. In that time, out of the hundreds of thousands who have served in the Royal Navy, Perisher has qualified just 1,165 Royal Navy officers and 365 officers of Commonwealth and other navies. Perisher has only two outcomes: pass or fail; and only one man, the Teacher, makes that judgement. Commander Fell served as Teacher from 1930–32 and 1935–37. He later wrote: 'The submariner must be a navigator, an electrician, a torpedo man, a gunnery type and even a bit of a plumber. He must know men and get on with them. He must use initiative and tact.'

Sladen and Fell eagerly took to their task, quickly arranging for a notice to be posted in all Royal Navy barracks, 'Volunteers required for dangerous and hazardous missions', realizing that this would attract only the most fearless of men.

The selection process was as rigorous as the training that was to follow. The volunteers came before Commander Sladen and two psychologists, who would ask personal questions in an effort to establish the reason for the men putting themselves forward. The object was to exclude the emotionally unbalanced because of failed love affairs, money problems or merely a death wish. Those initially selected would then face a full medical examination, after which only the most physically fit young men with a tough mental attitude would be selected for training at HMS *Dolphin*, the Royal Navy establishment at Fort Blockhouse, Gosport, home to the RN Submarine Service from the early 1900s and to the RN Submarine School.

The first and probably the most demanding part of that training involved mastering the use of the DSEA breathing set in *Dolphin*'s cylindrical diving tower, similar in shape to a large gasometer but filled with water. With the DSEA set in place, a nose clip painfully pinching the nostrils shut and while gripping the mouthpiece firmly between the teeth, each man would enter a watertight chamber at the bottom of the tower and the door would be closed behind him. Water would then be pumped into the chamber until it rose above the man's head, filling the chamber and equalling the pressure of the water above. At this stage, an overhead wheel within the chamber could be turned to open the escape hatch, enabling the man inside to swim slowly to the surface 39ft above. The claustrophobic effect of the chamber and the strange sensation of breathing through the mouthpiece took some getting used to. Those who were unable to cope quickly found themselves back at their previous posting, with no shame attached; there could be no room for failure under pressure.

Running concurrently with the selection and training of the men, but initially unknown to them, was the design and construction of their means of underwater transport, which would incorporate that all-important element, the explosive charge, it being the whole point of the exercise. Some small scraps of equipment had survived the Italian attack, and these, together with the underlying concept that this was to be a two-man torpedo, formed the basis of the British version, which became known as a 'chariot', and those who manned it 'charioteers'. To say that the starting point was from a low base is no exaggeration, as the prototype was a log of wood of the required diameter and cut to the required length of 20ft. To this would be gradually added the components to enable it to float upright, to carry two men and ancillary equipment, to dive and surface as required while being also navigable in the desired direction. The final requirement was the motive power, but initial tests were conducted by the simple expedient of having a motorboat tow the log at the optimum speed, later calculated to be 3 knots.

Initial testing of the log began at the Haslar testing tank, a concrete construction built originally for determining the performance characteristics of paraffin wax models of ships' hulls. As built in 1884, it was 540ft long, 20ft wide and 7.75ft deep, housed in a brick building at the Admiralty Experimental

Establishment, Gosport. From there it was on to Horsea Lake, a long narrow stretch of water near Portsmouth formed by the joining in 1889 of two lakes, Great and Little Horsea, to form a torpedo testing area. In 1905, the length was increased from 800 yards to 1,000 yards, but due to advances in torpedo range and technology, the facility had become all but obsolete by 1914, when it then became the home of the Royal Navy & Royal Engineer Training Facility, Portsmouth. Experiments with the log proved that the difference in buoyancy between the freshwater of the testing tank and the more buoyant seawater of Horsea Lake required the addition of more lead weights, but not before some startling results occurred as the charioteers riding on the log endeavoured to dive.

Sadly, despite all reasonable precautions being taken, several deaths occurred during the vigorous underwater training through which the volunteers went. The biggest danger was the blackouts suffered by divers after prolonged exposure to oxygen at depth, and while of no consolation to those who lost their lives, valuable lessons were learnt, enabling repeat mistakes to be avoided, with equipment and the operation thereof being adjusted as necessary. Commander Fell continued to put the men through their paces, while Commander Sladen was given the task of designing a new, lightweight, flexible diver's suit, to be made by HMS *Excellent*, the Royal Navy 'stone frigate' (shore establishment) on Whale Island, Portsmouth. Sladen approached Messrs Siebe Gorman and Company, manufacturers who were experienced in the production of heavy diving suits to which brass helmets were attached. Sladen followed the pattern of the helmet diver's dress – the body made of rubberized twill – simply replacing the cumbersome brass helmet with a standard army gas mask that was welded to the rubber neckband of the suit. The all-in-one suit had an opening at the stomach through which the diver would climb; the excess material was then folded and held tightly sealed by a metal clamp. Compared with the suits used by the Italian frogmen, this was a very crude arrangement, but a start had to be made somewhere. The first Siebe Gorman suits were ready to be put into use by the spring of 1942. Getting into these suits was no easy matter, and each diver would be allocated one, or sometimes two, dressers to help; the dressers were themselves often also qualified divers. For its 'watertight' properties, the Sladen suit was known to divers as the 'Clammy Death'.

The breathing apparatus recovered following the earlier Italian frogman attack at Gibraltar was similar to the British DSEA set used for escape from submarines. The new British specification called for up to six hours' endurance underwater without releasing tell-tale bubbles, and the only gas capable of meeting this requirement was oxygen. The Admiralty Diving Committee had decided to establish the headquarters of the Admiralty Experimental Diving Unit (AEDU) at Siebe Gorman's works at Tolworth, Surrey. Aware that oxygen was dangerous and could, if wrongly used, bring about poisoning, a team of experts set about solving the problems. The team consisted of Mr R.W.G. Davis, MA (Cantab), and the Chairman of Siebe Gorman, Sir Robert Davis, DSc (Hons) FRSA, together with Commander Sladen and Lieutenant Commander W.O. Shelford, the DSEA instructor at *Dolphin*.

This collaboration soon produced results, and by May 1942 the unique breathing apparatus was ready for use. For testing its practical application, a special unit was formed, consisting of instructors, medical officers and laboratory assistants, supervised by Professor J.B.S. Haldane, an acknowledged leader in DSEA technology. Here was perhaps the most concentrated and exhaustive diving programme ever undertaken, using volunteers as human guinea pigs, taking them beyond the limit of their endurance, to convulsions and unconsciousness. Despite all this, Sir Robert Davis was to recall: 'The young staff of the Unit showed great courage in submitting themselves cheerfully to these experiments. In spite of the risk and unpleasantness of the job, the experimental department was always a scene of cheerful activity.' Two medical officers would be on hand to render the volunteers immediate treatment as and when required, which was quite often. It is of interest to note here that the aluminium alloy used to construct the oxygen bottles was in short supply, and thus reliance had to be placed on the recovery of such metal from German aircraft shot down over Britain.

By means of trial and error, helped along by the arrival at Gosport of the remnants of two recovered *maiale*, progress was made, and the point reached where it was felt by Sladen and Fell that a working chariot could now be produced. Around this time, a request was put to the Admiralty to have a number of prototypes built and, with permission granted, the commission was given to Messrs Stothert & Pitt, crane manufacturers, who were at that time producing tanks for the British Army. In their factory at Bath in Somerset, a corner of the workshop floor was screened off with corrugated iron to maintain complete secrecy for the building of Job Nos 6590–6595. Only the most trustworthy employees were selected to carry out the work, each being sworn to secrecy and only allowed into the restricted area with a security pass.

Work began on the manufacture of the three sections that made up the cylindrical hull of the British human torpedo. The explosive warhead, the centre and tail sections were constructed of 3/32in non-magnetic steel, which were then bolted together to form what was, to all appearances, a large submarine torpedo of conventional shape. The three sections of the superstructure, all made of wood, were then added, creating buoyancy to keep the machine upright when submerged. In front of the driver, who would be sitting astride in an upright position, were the control instruments, installed behind a protective shield. In the centre, between the two divers, was the buoyancy tank, which was free-flooding. The valve on the top of the tank was opened to allow air to escape while water entered from holes at the base, thus allowing the machine to sink. Behind the second diver was the free-flooding bosun's locker, fixed to the hull by brass straps and used to carry magnets, rope and a net-lifting ram which was subsequently replaced by net-cutters.

The machine was painted olive green overall and, before final assembly, the internal parts were fitted. The tail section housed the 2hp (1.5kW) electric motor, manufactured by Mawdesley & Co., air bottles, air pump, rear trimming tank and the drum controller. The latter was manufactured by GEC and provided speed control (including reverse) for the propulsion motor. The centre section held thirty batteries arranged in two rows, plus the forward trimming tank. At the front was the detachable warhead, with 600lb (272kg) of high explosive (Torpex) in the centre, and on either side a buoyancy compartment to which lead weights could be added to obtain neutral buoyancy. On the outside of the warhead was the electric clock mechanism of the detonator, which could be set by the diver in up to ten increments of sixty minutes each.

Training continued for the volunteers, now reduced through selection or default to just sixteen. It should say here that many of those returned to their units for one reason or another had assisted greatly, through the experimental training they endured, in the understanding of what the mind and body – particularly the lungs – could survive underwater. Now for those sixteen came 'the Pot', described by one volunteer as being 'a diabolical contraption', at Siebe, Gorman's works at Tolworth, used to simulate the pressure underwater at depths of up to 150ft. For the volunteers who underwent the four months of experiments there, flaking-out sessions, caused by oxygen poisoning, were a common occurrence. However, their work, and that of the technicians and medical staff, determined conclusively that oxygen poisoning occurred if a diver breathed oxygen at depths greater than 30ft, equivalent to 14lb per square inch pressure. This became the maximum safe depth for oxygen-only diving and allowed chariot operations to proceed with confidence. And so, operations moved north from Fort Blockhouse to the sea lochs of the north-west coast of Scotland, where HMS *Titania* (see Notes) would become mother ship to the chariots and charioteers. The next phase would put them through their paces in an environment replicating that in which actual operations would be carried out. Enthusiasm was now to be tempered with the demand for the ultimate in technical efficiency. At this time, thoughts were beginning to focus on the selection of suitable enemy targets for the chariots, and the means by which they, with their short range, might be delivered within striking distance of those targets. A ride on The Shetland Bus perhaps?

Chapter 4

The Shetland Bus

Da wind flans in frae Fitful Head
Whaar dayset in a glöd
Hings ower da far haaf's wastern rim
Reeb'd red as yatlin blöd.[1]

When Germany launched Operation Weserübung, the invasion of Norway, on 9 April 1940, French and British troops and ships were sent to help the Norwegians. Their attempt to stem the tide of the invader's advance was in vain, with several coastal towns being bombed and destroyed by the Germans, and during April and May the British ships were forced to withdraw. A few weeks after the German occupation began, the first boats of an 'armada' of Norwegian fishing vessels and other boats began to arrive in Shetland, with some boats making several journeys carrying refugees across the North Sea. The islands that make up Shetland lie just over 100 miles north by northeast of mainland Scotland

---

[1] Verse from the poem 'Flans Frae Da Haaf', written in the Shetland dialect by Laurence Graham (1924–2009). Fitful Head is a headland and landmark at the southern tip of the Shetland mainland. The poem tells of the dangers of the sea and the feelings of those who wait for loved ones to return. 'Dayset' = sunset, 'Glöd' = glow, 'Far haaf's' = deep sea's, 'Reeb'd' = streaked, and 'Yatlin' = pure.

and extend for 60 miles north to south. Some 180 miles to the east lies Bergen, from where the Norwegian coast runs north for 120 miles and then north by northeast for almost a thousand miles into the Arctic Circle. From Lerwick the main town and port of Shetland in a typical fishing boat of that time, the nearest Norwegian landfall involved a voyage under favourable weather conditions of around twenty-four hours.

'The Shetland Bus' became the nickname given to a clandestine special operations group that established a permanent link between Shetland, Scotland and Nazi-occupied Norway from 1941 until the surrender of the German forces there on 8 May 1945. The service was operated initially by a large number of small fishing boats, the crews being men of the Norwegian coast: fishermen and sailors with detailed local knowledge. They came over shortly after the occupation, some with their own vessels and others with boats that were appropriated, legally or otherwise. The majority of these were young men in their 20s, some even younger. Many of them did several trips in the spring and summer of 1940, evacuating British soldiers who had been stranded in Norway after the unsuccessful Allied campaign, together with other British citizens living in Norway.

Crossings were mostly made during the winter months under the protective darkness of the longer nights to avoid the constant risk of discovery by German aircraft or patrol boats. Crews and passengers had to endure the rough North Sea conditions, with no lights to be shown on board or to be seen on shore, which added to the risks. The boats were all originally working fishing boats and kept up the pretence of that employment as the best form of open concealment from their actual purpose. For the same reason, the crews continued to look and act like fishermen as and when required. The boats were armed for anti-aircraft protection with light machine guns concealed in innocent-looking oil drums fixed to the deck.

To a casual observer, the fishing boats all appeared the same: two-masted wooden vessels, usually high in the bow and with a large wheelhouse aft. The bulwarks and upper works were painted white, with the hull not painted but its woodwork treated with linseed oil. Most of the vessels used were between 50 – 70ft long, with a beam of around 18ft and a draft of 8½ft. They had bunks for between six and eight men in the fo'c'sle and for two more in a small cabin aft. The hold amidships could carry up to 10 tonnes of arms, ammunition and explosives, and the wheelhouse – built on top of the engine casing – usually had a small chart-room opening off it and a galley behind that. With a top speed of 7 – 8 knots, they were slow by comparison with other vessels available at that time, but for sea-keeping ability, few boats of similar size could match them. The most noticeable feature of these Norwegian craft was the engine, a single-cylinder semi-diesel machine with a large reverberant exhaust pipe which poked out of the top of the wheelhouse and emitted a slow, solemn and very loud 'tonk-tonk-tonk'. This sound could be heard for miles in calm conditions, and would echo loudly around the steep sides of a Norwegian fjord. In a list of the vessel's strong points, stealth would not feature.

In late 1940, both the Secret Intelligence Service (SIS) and Special Operations Executive (SOE) Norwegian Naval Independent Unit established a base in Lerwick. They asked some of the skippers of the boats that were coming from Norway if they would return to deliver agents and bring others back to Shetland. This informal arrangement went on throughout the winter of 1940/41, but in early 1941 it was decided to establish a group of men and boats on a more formal basis to assist the SIS and SOE. The main purpose of the group was to transfer agents in and out of Norway and provide them with weapons, radios and other supplies. They would bring out Norwegians who feared arrest by the Germans and others who wished to volunteer to serve with the Allied forces. Sometimes the group would be involved in special operations, one such being Operation Title.

The man charged with forming this somewhat loose arrangement into a cohesive unit was Major Leslie H. Mitchell [see Notes], a British Army officer praised for his 'brilliant ideas, great charm, and irrepressible sense of humour'. He selected as his headquarters on Shetland, Flemington House, a comfortable, dilapidated farmhouse in the valley of Weisdale, surrounded by a plantation of stunted trees. The main building was large enough to accommodate the comings and goings of an unusual assortment of individuals, including British Army and naval officers and senior commanders, Norwegian naval personnel, the Norwegian Crown Prince, strong-willed Norwegian fishermen, agents, saboteurs and refugees. Second in command was Lieutenant David Howarth, RNVR [see Notes]. For his part of the operation, mainly concerning the boats and their crews, Howarth selected as his headquarters Lunna House, originally a large seventeenth-century laird's house, at Lunna Ness, with its little sheltered harbour of West Lunna Voe ('Voe' = a small bay). While the location was ideal for the boats, the lack of a slipway and other repair facilities meant that the boats initially had to be repaired at Malakoff's Boatyard in Lerwick. Later, Howarth moved the boats and crews to Scalloway, where William Moore & Son had a mechanic's workshop and where a new slipway was built, named after the Norwegian Crown Prince, Prince Olav. All ship repairs were carried out there, but Lunna Voe was still used as the setting-off point for special operations.

Howarth said of Lunna:

'I have always had a liking for bleak and lonely places, and perhaps it was on romantic grounds that I first determined that Lunna should be our base. The wild, desolate and deserted appearance of the place, and its remoteness suggested perfectly the smugglers' haunt of fiction. But I had to support my romance with reason. Luckily that was not too difficult. The house was to let, and it could accommodate thirty-five men. There were plenty of out-houses for stores, explosives and ammunition. The quay was built of great bocks of stone and had enough water for boats to lie alongside for six hours of the tide. The only other buildings in sight were a farm, a manse and an ancient church; and the bay was so placed that our boats could come and go on their errands without being seen by anyone, even the coastguards. The anchorage seemed to be safe, and when a few days later I brought one of the boats up to survey it I found the depth was just right from 4 to 5 fathoms.

'All these advantages seemed to well outweigh the disadvantage of the distance from Lerwick, which was our only source of supply, and of the indifferent road.

We reported to headquarters on the virtues of Lunna, answered the questions which convention compelled them to ask, and very soon leased the place furnished. This acquisition completed the material resources which we could foresee we should need during the coming winter. Lunna was to house the operational crews, with myself in charge, and the boats anchored here. Our office remained in Lerwick, where communications were more reliable and the navy and army headquarters were close at hand, so that the ciphers and other secret documents we kept were under better protection than we could have given them outside the town. Flemington was retained as a place where agents could be kept in seclusion while they waited for passage, and Mitchell continued to live there. Stocks of arms and explosives which we were to export were cached in a number of dumps throughout the islands, one of which was in the dungeon of the ruined medieval castle of the Earls of Zetland in the village of Scalloway. A day came at the end of July 1941 when the house was ready and the crews with five boats left Lerwick for the three-hour voyage to Lunna. When the boats were secured I brought the crews up to the house. They came in, took off their caps, wiped their feet and enquired, "Does the King of Shetland live here?"'

The long hours of daylight during the summer months severely curtailed the running of The Shetland Bus. Although weather conditions would be in their favour, the boats could be easily spotted by German planes flying patrols from Norwegian coastal bases out into the North Sea. Any ship sailing from the west towards the coast would be a prime target. At Scalloway, the summer was thus a time for the crews, their shore-based mechanics and shipwrights to repair the damage caused to the boats during the previous season's crossings and bring them up to a seaworthy condition ready to begin the process all over again as the days shortened. All work and no play makes Jack a dull boy, they say, and for the boat crews their leisure time was, to an alarming extent, taken up with pistol shooting in the rugged outdoor environment of the island. Nothing and no one was safe; anything that moved, and many things that did not, were fair game. Had the shooters' aim matched their enthusiasm and the number of rounds expended, then the island's rabbit population would have been quickly wiped out.

In October 1943, the old, slow fishing boats were replaced by three fast and well-armed submarine chasers named *Vigra*, *Hessa* and *Hitra*, a gift from the US Navy to The Shetland Bus operation on the instigation of Admiral Chester Nimitz, Commander-in-Chief of the US Pacific Fleet and a leading authority on submarines. These craft were 110ft long and powered by two 1,200hp diesel engines, giving the vessels a top speed of 22 knots (25 mph), with a normal cruising speed of 17 knots (20 mph). Sadly, prior to the arrival of these fast craft, forty-four crew members of The Shetland Bus service lost their lives through German attacks or the perils of the sea. Today, a memorial stone recording the names and deeds of these brave men stands at Scalloway, where a remembrance service is held annually, attended by a large contingent of Norwegians. By the end of the war, the group had made 198 trips to Norway in fishing boats and submarine chasers, Leif Larsen [see Notes 20] completing fifty-two of them. The Shetland Bus had transported 192 agents and 389 tonnes of weapons and supplies to Norway, and had brought out seventy-three agents and 373 refugees.

It was to be from these Norwegian seafarers and the boats of The Shetland Bus service, that in late October 1942 Leif Larsen with his crew of Bjørnøy, Strand, and Kalve and *Arthur*, the boat he had earlier 'repatriated' from Norway, were selected to play a major role in Operation Title. Larsen's 'passengers' were six Royal Navy divers selected by Commander Fell from his by now fully trained team of charioteers. *Arthur*'s special cargo was to be two of the chariots which had been brought to operational efficiency under the energetic direction of Commander Sladen.

Our story now moves over 700 miles south from Shetland to an event that took place on the island of Sark, one of the smaller Channel Islands, at the beginning of October, 1942. While at first sight this event, an Allied mission code named Operation Basalt, may appear to have no relevance to Operation Title, the connection will later become apparent.

Chapter 5

Operation Basalt

When it was announced by Hitler that the Channel Islands were to be invaded and occupied by German forces, Winston Churchill made the decision that, as they held no strategic importance to the Allied war effort, and to avoid unnecessary civilian casualties, no resistance was to be offered. An emergency programme of evacuation was promptly put into effect, large numbers of islanders and almost 80 per cent of the islands' schoolchildren being evacuated to the UK mainland.

On Friday, 28 June 1940, residents of the Channel Island of Sark watched as three German bombers passed overhead on their way to strike the larger neighbouring island of Guernsey. Thirty-four civilians were killed and a further thirty-three injured when the German planes bombed the harbour at St Peter Port, having mistaken for troops a row of lorries loaded with tomatoes awaiting export at the docks. After delivering two attacks on the harbour, the three aircraft individually attacked the Fruit Export Sheds, La Vassalerie, St Andrew and the area around Vazon. Some islanders have since said the incident could have been avoided if the demilitarization of the islands had been better communicated to the German military by the UK government. Two days after the bombing, German forces began landing on the Channel Islands: the start of a five-year occupation lasting until what is now celebrated annually there as Liberation Day, 9 May 1945. It was not long after landing that the Germans, using forced foreign labour, began a construction programme of fortification on a massive scale, totally out of proportion to the size and strategic importance of the islands. This was to form part of Hitler's 'impregnable' Atlantic Wall.

On the smaller island of Sark, where the residents had taken the decision to remain, civil authority rested in the hands of Sybil Hathaway, the Dame of Sark. A German-speaker herself, she encouraged the island's children to learn the language of the Nazi occupiers. Like many, however, she quietly resisted as best she could, listening at great personal risk to the BBC on an illegal radio, the Germans having confiscated all the other sets on the island. Although, through these illegal receivers, the islanders might learn something of what was going on in the wider world, the Allies had little intelligence about what was happening in the occupied Channel Islands. One thing that was clear from aerial reconnaissance was that the islands, which lie a few miles off the west coast of Normandy's Cotentin Peninsula, were being fortified. As for the conditions being endured by the many British subjects who lived on Jersey, Guernsey, Sark and the other smaller islands, little was known.

While it was never Britain's intention to retake the Channel Islands by military force, being hard-pressed to spare men or resources involved in more strategically important battles elsewhere, as early as July 1940, small groups of specially trained commandos began a series of pin-prick raids on the German forces stationed there. One of those raids, code named Operation

Basalt, wound up having an impact far beyond its minor though successful objective.

In the autumn of 1942, Major Geoffrey Appleyard was the commander of the Small Scale Raiding Force (No. 62 Commando) given the mission to land a dozen men on Sark to gather intelligence on the German presence on this small, 2-square-mile island. If possible, they were to return to England with prisoners for interrogation. Information concerning the German fortifications was specifically sought as being vital for any future Allied plans to invade and reoccupy Europe via its Atlantic coastline.

On the night of 3 October 1942, Appleyard and his men made their way to Sark in Motor Torpedo Boat (MTB) 334, known for some reason as 'Little Pisser', commanded by Lieutenant Freddie Bourne, RNVR. This small fast craft, 60ft long with a top speed of 33 knots, delivered the men of the raiding force undetected to within a short distance of the beach, which was then reached with the use of a Goatley boat. This was a collapsible boat, built for military use, having a wooden bottom, canvas sides and a recommended capacity of ten men. It would take two men around two minutes to assemble and, weighing only 330lb (150kg), could be carried by four men. The boat was designed by, and named after, Fred Goatley of Saunders-Roe and used in a number of commando and other operations by British forces during the Second World War. Upon landing, the raiders scaled the Hog's Back, a promontory jutting out into the sea, and began their search for Germans.

Very little information was available in advance of the raid to assist Appleyard. Indeed, during their training for the raid, the group was forced to map out the operation using a recreational hiking guide to the island, along with home movies from Appleyard's own family, which had holidayed on Sark before the war. Low-grade photo reconnaissance showed what seemed to be a machine-gun nest, but which turned out to be a nineteenth-century cannon.

The first group of buildings the raiders searched was empty, but the second, an isolated house known as La Jaspellerie, yielded better results. They broke in and awakened the sleeping resident, a British woman, Mrs Frances Pittard, who, upon seeing the uniformed men with their faces blackened, imagined them to be firemen and asked if the house was on fire. Once it became clear that the men were British soldiers, Mrs Pittard was keen to assist. She offered them cups of tea, showed them local maps and told them where they could find German troops nearby. She gave them recent Channel Island newspapers which would reveal to the British government some of the war crimes taking place in the islands, with news on the deportation of civilians to Germany.

In the annexe of the nearby Dixcart Hotel, a small group of German engineers, recently arrived on Sark, were asleep. A single sentry patrolled outside. One of Appleyard's men, a Danish commando named Anders Lassen, was ordered to kill the lookout, which he did silently using his commando knife. Lassen would go on to earn the Military Cross and two bars before being awarded a posthumous Victoria Cross during the Italian campaign. The five Germans inside the building were sleeping soundly, their weapons having been left in the hall outside their rooms. They were roused and taken outside in various stages of undress, where Appleyard gave the orders for their hands to be bound and to shoot any who tried to escape. Upon realizing this was not the long-expected Allied invasion but only a small raiding party, the prisoners began shouting and resisting their captors. In the resulting confusion, some shots were fired. There were over 300 German soldiers on Sark, many of them in the neighbouring Stocks Hotel, less than 100 metres away, so, with the alarm now raised, Appleyard and his party beat a hasty retreat. In the end, only one prisoner remained in the hands of the commandos, Obergefreiter [Senior lance-corporal] Hermann Weinreich, commander of the small group of engineers. The commandos dashed with their captive down into a wooded ravine and up the other side, desperate to get back to the Hog's Back and 'Little Pisser', their getaway boat, before the German garrison turned out in force. Time was of the essence as the commandos had already been on the island for some three hours and the boat needed the cover of darkness for a safe evacuation. They made it down the cliff just in time.

On the way back to England, the commandos discussed what had just transpired on Sark, with Lassen expressing his concern that the shooting of the Germans, whose hands had been bound, could be seen as a war crime. He even suggested that they return to the island and remove the ropes from any bodies they left behind, but this idea was rejected by Appleyard.

The party made its way back to the safety of Portland harbour, where the raid was considered a huge success, Churchill being quick to give Appleyard his personal congratulations.

Back on Sark, the waking Germans found a scene of carnage, with several of their soldiers dead. The Nazi propaganda machine swiftly denounced the British commandos as war criminals, pointing as proof to prisoners being shot in cold blood with their hands tied.

Following the raid, suspicion fell on Mrs Pittard as one who may have helped the commandos with information. She was arrested and jailed for a time on Guernsey. She returned to Sark after a few months, but only for a brief visit. Reprisals were carried out against the people of Sark, including Mrs Pittard, who, like many fellow islanders, was deported to a detention camp in Germany. With the war's end, some suspected that she had fallen victim to German vengeance, but she survived, returned to Sark and lived there until her death in 1960.

Immediately upon arrival on the British mainland, the commandos' hostage, Obergefreiter Weinreich, was taken for interrogation to the notorious 'London Cage'. Also known as 'Connor McCracken's room', the London Cage was an MI19 prisoner-of-war facility during and after the Second World War used to interrogate captured Germans, including SS personnel and members of the Nazi Party. The unit was located within numbers 6, 7, and 8 Kensington Palace Gardens, London. The British systematically interrogated all of its prisoners of war, and a 'cage' for interrogation of prisoners was established in 1940 in each command area of the United Kingdom, manned by officers trained by Lieutenant Colonel Alexander P. Scotland, OBE, the head of the Prisoner of War Interrogation Section (PWIS) of the Intelligence Corps (Field Security Police). After their interrogation at the cages, the prisoners were sent to various PoW camps both in the UK and overseas.

According to reports, Obergefreiter Weinreich provided a great deal of useful intelligence regarding the German defensive fortifications, not only on Sark but also along the French coast where he and his men had previously been stationed. The newspaper given to Appleyard by Mrs Pittard, *The Guernsey Star and Evening Express*, provided the British government with evidence of the war crimes being committed on the islands. A proclamation signed by Oberst Knackfuss, Feldkommandant, stated:

> 'All male civilians (i) not born on the Channel Islands; (ii) not permanently resident there – between the ages of 16 and 60, have been deported to Germany together with their families for forced labour. The deportation took place last week at the shortest notice and 900 men were conscripted from Guernsey, 400 are still to go and it is expected there will be more from Jersey. Eleven men of Sark were warned to be ready to go last week. Two committed suicide and only nine left.'

More significantly, the raid led to Hitler's infamous *Kommandobefehl*, or Commando Order, issued just two weeks later on 18 October 1942. Furious over what had happened on Sark, the Führer decreed that, with immediate effect, any Allied commando captured, whether in uniform or not, was to be treated as a terrorist and summarily executed. The full text of the order appears in the Notes section at the end of this book. The success of Operation Basalt thus proved to be something of a Pyrrhic victory, its bearing on Operation Title slowly unfolding.

Chapter 6

Preparations Under Way

In his biography of Admiral Sir Max Horton, Rear Admiral William Scott Chalmers describes, in just two paragraphs, the preparations for Operation Title as follows:

'Several "chariots" were ready for service by the summer of 1942. As the *Tirpitz* had not emerged from the Norwegian fjords, Max, feeling that "a chance lost in war may never recur", decided to send two chariots in a Norwegian fishing boat to Trondheim, where the *Tirpitz* spent most of her time. On arrival near Trondheim Fjord, the chariots were to be put over the side and towed underneath the fishing vessel, which would then go up the fjord hoping to pass through German control with false passports. It was planned she should reach a point about eight miles from the *Tirpitz* shortly after dark, when the charioteers would emerge from their hiding place and ride their machines to the target. As soon as they had gone, the fishing boat was to scuttle herself.

'The Norwegian fishing vessel *Arthur* was selected for the task. She was commanded by Skipper L.A. Larsen [see Notes] and manned by a Norwegian crew. The charioteers, all British, were commanded by Sub Lieutenant W.R.

Brewster, RNVR. The Commander-in-Chief Home Fleet, Sir John Tovey, approved the project and arranged that one of his battleships should play the part of *Tirpitz* in a dress rehearsal. The ship was moored head and stern near the steep-to shore of a lonely Scottish loch in the same manner as *Tirpitz* at Trondheim. All the "stage props" required to complete the scene, such as nets, mines and other obstructions, were placed in their correct positions relative to the target. Fishing vessels for rescue and shore parties representing the Norwegian "underground" were briefed for the task of helping prisoners to escape. The crews selected for the assault had already been trained and exercised to the limit of physical endurance. Nothing was left to chance and several rehearsals were required before Horton was satisfied.'

Although Chalmers covers the essence, the details deserve to be recorded more fully. One important aspect of the whole operation, giving it the best possible chance of success, was to protect it so far as possible with a cloak of legitimacy. To this end, a Norwegian crew would be sailing a Norwegian fishing vessel loaded with a cargo of peat, ostensibly from an off-shore Norwegian island but readily sourced from Shetland, for delivery to a consignee in Trondheim. To deceive the curious and satisfy the German controls through which the boat would inevitable have to pass, every document, of which there were many, had to be authentic or such good forgeries as to survive the closest scrutiny. SOE and SIS agents collected information about everything which might impact the effectiveness of the charioteers. They gathered details of topography, meteorology (daylight and darkness hours, winds, temperatures, snow and frost), oceanography and also hydrography. This was particularly important, as water density can vary not just between fresh and sea water (as the charioteers had discovered) but also at different temperatures, which could affect buoyancy and the vital ability of the chariots to remain submerged at a particular depth. They also collected information on other warships anchored in the vicinity and the nature of the booms protecting them, details which could not be gained without difficulty and danger.

A great deal of reliance had to be placed on boats coming across from Norway, their crews bringing up-to-date papers, which could be forged to match the cover story, together with the latest news on the German patrols, minefields and areas designated by them as prohibited to commercial traffic. There must be no evidence whatever that the vessel had come from the British side of the North Sea, so every piece of equipment of English origin had to be taken out, including food and clothing. On a personal note, the crew would require the correct identity documents which would need to match the crew list. Finally, the ship's papers recording ownership, tonnage and port of registry had to be forged, as did the ship's log showing all previous ports of call and German patrol points passed, with appropriate stamps and signatures.

In October 1941, Leif Larsen was the engineer on *Nordsjøen*, which was minelaying in the Edøyfjord. The vessel sank in a heavy gale on its return journey, but the crew were able to make their way to land. Some of them, including the ship's skipper, then disappeared. Larsen took charge of the remainder, leading them for over 100 miles through occupied territory to Ålesund, where he stole the fishing boat *Arthur* (see Notes) and sailed it back to Lerwick. For this he received the Distinguished Service Medal. *Arthur* was the vessel then selected to carry the chariots and divers to Norway, for which purpose, on top of being completely stripped of anything English, several major modifications were required to fulfil its role in the operation. Firstly, the means by which the chariots were to be attached to the underside of the hull for the transit up Trondheim Fjord had to be fitted. Stout eyebolts were fitted to the keel about one-third of the boat's length from the stem. To these were attached two steel cables, each having a shackle at the end which would later be connected to the chariot warhead's towing fitment. The free ends were brought inboard and stopped to the main shroud until required. As it was crucial to the whole operation, the strength and integrity of this fitting left nothing to chance. Had there been a Lloyd's Register specification for such a fitting, it would have qualified A1+.

Secondly, the means had to be sorted by which the chariots and warheads were to be lifted off the ship and into the water. The boom for the mainsail, attached to the mast by a goose-neck fitting, had to be strengthened. The boom, which doubled as a cargo-handling derrick, could in normal circumstances cope with the odd sling full of barrels, bags and bales, or more recently, cases and crates of arms and ammunition. Its safe working load, however, was insufficient to cater for the 2-tonne load which a chariot presented, so modifications had to be made to both it and the topping lift. For the voyage across the North Sea, the warheads were to be carried in the hold, hidden under the cargo of bagged peat. The chariots themselves were to be carried on top of the hatch, hidden under tarpaulins, and for this the hatch battens had to be strengthened and cradles specially made to keep the chariots from shifting in transit.

Next to be dealt with was the question of where, in such a small boat, space was to be found that would conceal from close German inspection six Royal Navy divers and their not inconsiderable amount of equipment. In practical terms, as the ship was conventionally configured, such space did not exist, and so space had somehow to be made. A false bulkhead was built across the breadth of the ship, from deck to deckhead, which provided a 3ft gap between the hold and the engine room. Using old timbers, fixed with old nails, which were then treated to a coat of grease and grime, the false bulkhead blended in with the surrounding engine room space so as to be indistinguishable from the original hold bulkhead. Access to this claustrophobic cavity was via a small opening on the engine room side which to any observer looked like the electrical circuit switchboard, which function it actually served. So cunning was the construction that the only means by which this cavity could be detected was by a comparison of internal and external measurements. Not even a thorough German search would go to these lengths.

While every preparation was in place for the operation itself, as much thought and planning went into the means by which an escape for the ten men might subsequently be made. It was always intended that *Arthur* should be scuttled after it had completed its role as a means of transport to the chariot drop-off point. In practical terms, it would have been impossible for it to reverse its course and hope to return to Shetland. Detonating a charge within the hull was not an option, so the plan was for large holes to be drilled with augers provided and for the seacocks to be opened. Some of the party cast doubt on these measures being sufficient to sink it successfully, so to appease them, extra ballast was loaded, but without any calculation being made as to its possible efficacy. Thereafter, the plans were in the hands of SOE-appointed agents in Norway. 'Lark' was the code name for the group that had been sent from the United Kingdom to Trondheim as part of the preparations for a possible Allied invasion of Norway. Lark developed into the main organization for the SOE in the Trøndelag district, and became the effective leadership of Milorg, the Norwegian resistance movement, in the region. Lark started its operations in Trøndelag in February 1942, when the group's mission was to start training men in weapons and guerrilla tactics. Initially, however, Lark was almost solely occupied with plans to sink the *Tirpitz*.

The original SOE contact in Trondheim, Odd Sørli, went over to Scalloway to advise the men of the escape plans Lark had put in place for them. After the attack, the four charioteers were to land within a certain stretch of the south shore of the fjord and make their way a short distance inland to a road which ran parallel to the shore. The road was to be patrolled by Lark members who would have a car ready to take the four straight to the Swedish frontier, 120 miles away, before dawn and before the time fuses of the warheads had exploded under *Tirpitz* and put the whole district in uproar. If this rendezvous failed, the four were to make for a certain conspicuous hill, where they could hide in thick woods during the day after the attack. They were to meet local agents on the bare summit of the hill the following evening. As by that time escape from the area by car would be impossible, the agents would guide the men across country on foot to the safety of neutral Sweden.

The six remaining men, after scuttling *Arthur*, were to row ashore to a second rendezvous, where cars would be waiting for them. If that meeting failed, they were to meet the four charioteers on the hilltop the following night. Finally, if all else failed, or if a landing had to be made in a different part of the fjord, the agents had sorted out a number of cross-country routes to the Swedish border that could be undertaken by small parties. In case they did have to walk to Sweden, all hands were issued with rucksacks, rations and suitable clothing, and route maps printed on silk.

A notice posted by Commanders Sladen and Fell in all Royal Navy barracks called for volunteers for dangerous and hazardous missions. Just how dangerous these missions might be is demonstrated by the following extract from the plans for Operation Title. To say that 'these four men will probably ... become prisoners of war' was rather optimistic:

TOP SECRET FILE HS2/202   12.9.1942
TITLE   Plans for the operation

(h) Whilst it is realised that these four men will probably not escape and will become prisoners of war, we wish to do all we can for them without endangering the LARK organisation.

While all these preparations were under way, Commander Fell had the charioteers relocate to the north west coast of Scotland in an isolated area well away from prying eyes and in waters more akin to those that might be encountered in operational conditions. From a log of wood and a group of strong swimmers – volunteers all, with scant regard for their own mortality – was being developed the means by which 'The Beast' was to be challenged.

Chapter 7

Scotland – and Beyond

U pon arrival in Scotland, the charioteers reported on board the newly recommissioned *Titania* (Captain H.R. Conway) lying in the Clyde. Known as 'Tites' throughout the submarine service, *Titania* was a depot ship of longstanding, having acted as a broody hen over submarine flotillas on the China and Mediterranean stations before the war. Those who 'enjoyed' the facilities on board would, if in a generous frame of mind, describe them as 'adequate'. Within a few days, it weighed anchor and proceeded westward down the Clyde estuary, round the Mull of Kintyre, then north past Rum, Eigg, Skye and Muck, through the Little Minch and into Loch Erisort, not far from Stornoway on the Isle of Lewis. In a position near the head of the loch, 'Tites' anchored and prepared for a long stay in what was to be known as Port D, a wild and lonely spot.

Commander Fell had travelled north in charge of the charioteers and was immediately implementing his plans for the establishment of an operational training base here and the prompt recommencement of training. Emphasis was to be on extending underwater endurance, initially using the adapted log prototype chariot, *Cassidy*. The nickname came from the limping cowboy hero of Saturday matinee western film fame, Hopalong Cassidy. The usual drill with *Cassidy* was for two divers to enter the water, discover if and where their suits were leaking, then, if not too wet and miserable, haul themselves astride. The towing motorboat would then go ahead, and when the appropriate signal was given, the diver riding as Number One would open the main ballast-vent, releasing the air and causing the machine to dive. After about fifteen or twenty minutes of being towed underwater, he would bring *Cassidy* to the surface again.

While the first three classes of charioteers were put through their paces at Port D, Commander Sladen, who had remained in Portsmouth, continued the recruitment programme while chasing, with as much diplomacy as he could muster, the first mechanical models of the chariot and the new diving gear. Eventually, and with little advance warning, Sladen turned up at Fort Blockhouse with the first powered chariot, which was promptly named the 'Real One'. There was the same trouble with manhandling it into the water as there had always been with *Cassidy*, but there the likeness was going to end. It would be easy, or so everyone thought, to just sit astride and drive along.

Final tests were made on the 'Real One', the pumps were run, the hydroplanes and rudder were found to answer and the high-pressure air bottles were full. Perfect. It was at this point that Commander Sladen sprang the surprise of the afternoon. 'Get dressed,' he ordered one of the divers, 'and get me into one of those suits.' Sladen was never one to ask his men to do something he was not prepared to do himself. One or two may have doubted the wisdom of what Sladen was about to do, as he had not used the suit or breathing apparatus more than half-a-dozen times. However, nobody argued with him and, not without some difficulty, his huge, rugby player's size frame was forced into an ordinary size suit and they were ready to start. With the two divers sat astride, Sladen acting as Number One, the machine moved off under its own power and, after much fiddling with the controls and the use of some choice sailor-speak, the 'Real One' was officially baptized.

The next day, Fort Blockhouse was visited unannounced by Rear Admiral (Submarines) Admiral Sir Max Horton, accompanied by Admiral Ernest J. King, chief naval officer of the US Navy, for whom a demonstration was laid on. In the hands of two senior diving officers, Warren and Grant, the 'Real One' behaved perfectly, diving and surfacing, answering rudder and hydroplanes as requested; all-in-all, a perfect performance. Nearly everybody seemed pleased, most were impressed, but it was apparent that Admiral King was not among the latter – and probably not among the former either. It is likely the American admiral, being used to dealing with warships on a large scale, failed to appreciate the potential for such a small submersible device to make any significant impact in the grand scheme of things. After a brief inspection of men and machine, the visitors headed back to London, while Sladen treated his two divers to lunch and a well-deserved beer. With the excitement of the day over, preparations were immediately made for the 'Real One' to be transported to Port D in company with the two divers, Warren and Grant, and the fourth class of recruits. Sladen stayed behind to oversee the production of another two machines, which, when ready, went straight up north. Here they were most welcome, for by the time they arrived, training was so far advanced that restlessness among the diving teams was beginning to set in. The appearance of the new machines quickly quietened the querulous.

Training was designed to bring about such expertise and familiarity with suit, breather and machine that it should become second nature, somewhat akin to driving a car. Charioteering was always going to be a cold, wet and miserable experience, with discomfort rather than danger being the perceived bugbear. It could only be by constant exposure to these elements that a diver would eventually accept them as normal: the risks went with the job. At this point it might be quite relaxing for the charioteers to glide along 20ft below the surface at a comfortable 1½ knots, admiring the underwater world in the clear waters of the loch. It would then be that suddenly, and without warning, the machine would plunge to the bottom. The divers would be driven to the point of madness by the pressure on their eardrums and with their lungs caving in for want of oxygen. In the buoyant saltwater alongside *Titania*, the chariots would be trimmed accordingly, but when that trim met a patch of less buoyant freshwater from one of the many burns that streamed down the hillsides to empty into the loch, a downward plunge was inevitable. It was not without good reason that the notice which appeared earlier in those naval barracks called for volunteers for 'dangerous and hazardous missions'. Divers would regularly lose consciousness at depths below 40ft, and it says much for the volunteers that, although 75 per cent of them passed out at one time or another, they continued with the job.

Once the requisite expertise and familiarity had been achieved, the divers moved on to dealing with such tasks as would be encountered in operational situations, chief of which involved defensive nets. An assortment of nets (large, deep, anti-submarine mesh and smaller, shallow, anti-torpedo mesh) was laid in the loch, through, under or over which the charioteers had to navigate, honing their skills against the experience of the Boom Defence Force brought in specifically for that purpose. It soon became apparent that what might stop a submarine or torpedo in its tracks was no obstacle to a chariot in the right hands. By far the biggest problem was to discover the best way of getting under a target to secure the chariot's warhead. After various methods were tried, unsuccessfully and with alarming and dangerous results, the head-on approach was chosen. By this method, the chariot would submerge some way from the target and drive towards it at the same depth as the target's draught until it hit or began to pass beneath. Within a week of the first successful practice attack being made by this method, everyone was using it and proving it to be 'easy'. There now began to grow a demand to put all this training into effect, with both Sladen and Fell canvassing higher authority for an operational opportunity. It was Sladen who travelled to Northways, Portsmouth, and Shetland to interview, plead, suggest and plan. Fell remained in *Titania*, dealing with the problem of a highly trained group of men for whom the lack of opportunity to put their training into action was becoming increasingly unacceptable.

Then it happened, as it does in the navy; a 'buzz' went round that an operation was on the cards, with teams to be selected soon. Standards inevitably rose, and it was accepted by Sladen and Fell that something more difficult than anything encountered to date had to be introduced into the training regime, something more closely replicating what might prove to be the real thing. Following a request to Rear Admiral (Submarines) Northways along these lines, orders came for the

Erisort base to be dismantled. *Titania* was to weigh anchor and proceed to a new base, its location known only to its skipper, Captain Conway, and the two commanders. The new location, code name Port HHZ, was to be Loch Cairnbawn, a sea loch which opens into Eddrachillis Bay on the Scottish mainland, due east of Stornoway and between Cape Wrath to the north and Ullapool to the south. Waiting for the visitors was the subsidiary depot ship HMS *Alecto* and a tender vessel, the drifter HMS *Easter Rose.*

Very shortly after *Titania* dropped anchor, it was followed into Loch Cairnbawn by the recently commissioned King George V-class battleship HMS *Howe.* Moored close to the shore and quickly surrounded by layers of anti-submarine netting, *Howe* was to be the charioteers' new target, with a more challenging draught of 29ft 6in plus a crew on full alert. Hydrophones, a patrol boat and Aldis signalling lamps doubling up for searchlights helped to cast the dice heavily against the attackers, as did *Howe*'s foreknowledge of the night and approximate time of the practice attacks. Despite these precautions, the score was four–nil to the attackers at the end of night one, and a two-all draw after night two. The third night, *Howe*'s last before departure for Arctic convoy duty, brought a stark reminder of the dangers, even in practice, of these attack manoeuvres. One diver, Sub Lieutenant J. Grogan, lost consciousness when his chariot was under the target, leaving the other diver, Able Seaman 'Geordie' Worthy, to take the controls and, with great difficulty and skill, reach the surface. Despite one of the dinghies being immediately on hand to render assistance, Grogan was dead. As a great character and first-class charioteer, Grogan's loss was keenly felt by the rest of the team and his death a cause of great concern to Sladen and Fell.

Autumn 1942 saw the coming together of various circumstances that inexorably led to the launch of a mission against Churchill's 'Beast'. Each component had a vital role to play, with perhaps the first being the appointment of Captain Sir Claud Barrington Barry to Rear Admiral [Submarines] as successor to Sir Max Horton. Barry's career to date as a successful submariner in the First World War would ensure a continuation of backing right from the top for Commanders Sladen and Fell and their team of charioteers. Next came the Norwegian skipper, Leif Larsen, champing at the bit for an opportunity to strike a blow for his occupied country. He had long wanted to see an end to *Tirpitz*, to him a symbol of the Nazi regime there, but was at a loss as to how he could do so with his Shetland Buses. He visited the powers that be in London in an effort to drum up business, pointing out that the coming winter with its long, dark nights was the open season for these little boats and their clandestine operations across the North Sea to the Norwegian coast. Then it was the turn of SOE and their agents in Norway, the Lark organization, part of the larger Norwegian resistance, to add their ingredient to the mixture. Lark had been monitoring the movements of *Tirpitz* since its arrival in Norwegian waters, keeping SOE up to date with its comings and goings and the defensive measures around the mighty warship wherever and whenever it moored. When it was then put to Larsen that he, with one of his boats, might be the means by which a secret weapon could be brought within striking distance of *Tirpitz*, he did not hesitate to say 'Yes'.

So it was that Larsen and *Arthur* made their way to Port HHZ to join the charioteers and examine the means by which a blow against the 'Beast' could best be dealt. With so many details to be thrashed out, it was fortunate that Larsen quickly fitted into the charioteers' team and their ways of thinking and working. Admiral Barry himself paid a visit and, to Larsen's great consternation, actually came on board *Arthur*. Larsen was not at his most relaxed when having to don a uniform and speak to men with 'scrambled egg' on the cap peaks, but he soon found himself taking part in what he later described as 'a homely conversation with a very pleasant gentleman'. Then it was down to business and the new training programme, which began with the all-important question as to how the chariots were to be towed by *Arthur*. The trials with them towed astern proved unsatisfactory, so the cables were shortened, and the chariots hung directly under the vessel's hull. From the charioteers in training, the final selection was made of six men in two crews of two, plus one crew in reserve who were to act as dressers for the important task of helping the divers into their suits and breathing apparatus. The six were Sub Lieutenant 'Jock' Brewster in command, with Able Seaman 'Jock' Brown as his No. 2; Sergeant Don Craig (RE), with Able Seaman Bob Evans as his No. 2; and Able Seamen Malcolm Causer and Billy Tebb as dressers/reserve divers.

The first full-scale trial took place in mid-October, this time with HMS *Rodney* as the target. The battleship was at that time based at Scapa Flow, between operations, a veteran of the Norwegian campaign and having earlier played a major role in the sinking of the German battleship *Bismarck*, sister ship to *Tirpitz*.

Eleven men sailed aboard *Arthur* – four crew, six charioteers and Commander Fell – into a deserted bay in the Summer Isles at the mouth of Loch Broom, where the chariots were hoisted out and slung beneath the hull. The tow then began back towards the loch where HMS *Rodney* lay, surrounded by three layers of wire nets. It was midnight when *Arthur* stopped engines at the place agreed for the release of the two chariots, several miles from the anchorage, and without delay the charioteers set off. They completed what turned out to be a most successful attack, cutting their way through two layers of net and sliding under the third before securing two warheads to *Rodney*'s hull. Despite the duty watch on deck, who were aware an attack was to be made, the charioteers had made their way in and out unobserved. Had this been the real thing, an audit of the Royal Navy fleet the next morning would have flagged up a shortage of one battleship. Further attacks were made, and wrinkles ironed out until 'Tiny' Fell announced himself satisfied that, so far as he was concerned, training at Loch Cairnbawn was complete. It was time for the selected charioteers, along with Larsen, *Arthur* and its crew, to move up to Shetland for a final short spell of training in surroundings even more closely resembling those which they were shortly to encounter.

The mission to sink *Tirpitz*, which had been given the code name Operation Title, was now finally on. The 'Beast' was located at anchor in Fættenfjord, a narrow cul-de-sac of water at the far eastern end of Trondheimsfjord. To reach *Tirpitz*, let alone sink it, presented a huge challenge in itself.

Chapter 8

Sink the *Tirpitz*

'The best laid schemes o' mice and men gang aft agley.'
(Robert Burns, 1785)
'De beste planene til mus og menn går ofte galt.'
(Norwegian translation of the above)

At the beginning of 1942, Churchill had asked the Chiefs of Staff what was being done to emulate the exploits of the Italians in Alexandria harbour. By the end of October that same year, Churchill had his question answered in the form of Operation Title. This SOE-led mission to sink the *Tirpitz* had begun with an idea that was turned into a reality in a very short space of time when three essential elements came together. Thanks largely to the efforts of Commanders Sladen and Fell, the chariots and divers had reached the required level of operational efficiency. Then, under Major Mitchell and Lieutenant Howarth, the operation of The Shetland Bus had been turned from a loose arrangement into an organized service, with men and boats better prepared for the dangerous North Sea crossings. Finally, the co-operation between the SOE Norwegian Section and Lark, the Norwegian resistance movement in the Trøndelag district, provided accurate, up-to-the-minute intelligence on the movements and location of *Tirpitz*.

Throughout this book, the author's desire has been to let the men and their records speak for themselves, and so, to this end, the following extract from the SOE report describing how the attempt on *Tirpitz* came together is included verbatim. It is dated just three weeks after the operation began:

'SN/2048

'16.Nov.42

'MOST SECRET
'ATTEMPT on "TIRPITZ"
'OPERATION TITLE – OCTOBER 1942

'In the middle of June 1942, SOE were approached by Admiral (Submarines) through Captain Lord Ashbourne [see Notes 3] RN and asked if it was possible to co-operate in a plan to attack the battleship TIRPITZ while she was lying at AASENFJORD 66o33'N 10o58'E in TRONDHEIMFJORD. An immediate reply was made that every effort would be made [to] render all assistance possible. Under Sir Charles Hambro's and Major General Gubbins' orders full responsibility was given to Colonel Wilson [see Notes 28], the Norwegian Section.

'THE FIRST PLAN

'After various consultations a plan, dated 26.Jun.42 was drafted, and a copy transmitted by code to STOCKHOLM with instructions to send a courier to TRONDHEIM.

This plan involved SOE co-operation in the following particulars:-

(a) Transport of operational party and their equipment from Shetland to a small island 63°48'N 8°50'E north of Froya due west of entrance to TRONDHEIMFJORD.

(b) Transfer of party of 2 or 3 men to a local fishing boat obtained by "Lark" organisation. The fishing boat to tow equipment through controls and unship them in mid-TRONDHEIMFJORD south-west of TAUTRA (approximately 63°32'N 10°32'E).

(c) Operation to be carried out towards beginning of October.

A local boat and its owner were named and passwords given to STOCKHOLM for the courier. After some unavoidable delay the courier left STOCKHOLM on 26.Jul.42. He did not return from TRONDHEIM until 4.Sep.42. It had taken him some weeks to get in touch with the owner of the fishing boat named, who had unfortunately refused to consider the project. The SOE leader of the "Lark" organisation, however, advocated sending a fishing craft direct through from the United Kingdom, equipped with false papers which would take it through the enemy control.

'Meanwhile steps had been taken to select a boat suitable for the transport of the men and equipment from

SHETLAND to TAUTRA. The support of Admiral (Submarines) secured the release to SOE of "Andholmen" in Iceland (and subsequently three other boats of a similar type.) It was intended to use the "Andholmen" for transport purposes since she was stronger than the other SOE boats in SHETLAND.

'THE SECOND PLAN

'The adverse report from STOCKHOLM necessitated an immediate and radical change of plan. The possibility of carrying out the whole operation from SHETLAND using MFV "Arthur" and not "Andholmen" was put under investigation on 8.Sep.42. "Arthur" was selected since her make and build were more suitable to the revised plan of running right into TRONDHEIMFJORD. Her skipper Quartermaster Leif Larsen D.S.M. who was in London at the time, immediately volunteered to take the boat in.

'Under the new plan it was decided to send over two "Chariots" with two pair[s] of specialists and two dressers, making six British officers and ratings. The two chariots were to be carried on deck until "Arthur" was north of Froya, when they were to be transferred to the towing gear. The plan was then for "Arthur" to run through the controls with the chariots in tow and with the six men concealed in a special hiding place hollowed out of the cargo of peat. This cargo was necessary in order to give the impression that the boat was on its lawful occasions.

'On 12.Sep.42 the necessary particulars of the second plan were sent by code to STOCKHOLM, setting out the co-operation required from the "Lark" organisation in securing the escape of both the RN personnel and the skipper and crew of "Arthur". Specimens of the papers for falsifying were also asked for and passwords, signals (both W/T and BBC) set out. The courier, owing to various circumstances, did not leave STOCKHOLM for TRONDHEIM until 23.Sep.42.

'The "Lark" W/T operator had previously crossed into SWEDEN after training a local operator. As no communication was being obtained from "Lark" station, he was halted in STOCKHOM and sent back on 28.Sep.42, while another W/T set, despatched from London, was sent over the border from STOCKHOLM by another courier.

'In co-operation with Admiral (Submarines) "Arthur" was tested and fitted with towing gear. A crew of four, including Larsen[,] was selected and sailed "Arthur" to the mainland, returning to LUNNA VOE with the RN personnel, six in all, on 3.Oct.42. Signal plans were worked out and all other arrangements made.

It is important to record that all this planning was taking place when the TIRPITZ was absent from the target area. Information received on 20.Jul.42 reported the battleship at BOGENFJORD near NARVIK where, except for short sorties, she remained up until at least 22.Oct.42. Despite this it was decided to press on with preparations for the execution of the plan in the faint hope that the TIRPITZ would return to TRONDHEIMFJORD by the beginning of November. This was considered to be the latest period when the operation could take place on account of water temperatures.

'FINAL ARRANGEMENTS

'The 'Lark' leader had himself arrived in STOCKHOLM at the beginning of October and local intelligence was supplied by him. When the courier from TRONDHEIM followed him with the necessary papers, he was flown over to LEUCHARS escorted by Mr E M Neilson, Head of the Norwegian Section of the SOE Branch in STOCKHOLM, arriving there on 7.Oct.42. The two were flown direct to Shetland, where the final arrangements were made to fix all the possible details, including the briefing of the skipper of "Arthur", and the briefing of the combined party in the two escape routes that were suggested for the four specialists and for the two dressers and the crew of "Arthur".

'The "papers" most meticulously prepared by Station 15 (Major C B Ince) were also flown to Shetland. All preparations were complete and the operation ready to move by 10.Oct.42. The TIRPITZ was still in BOGENFJORD. On 16.Oct.42 it was decided by Admiral (Submarines) to postpone the operation until 25.Oct.42, from which date "Arthur" was ready to sail. Meanwhile, wireless connection had been established with the "LARK" Station and signals were exchanged.

"'TIRPITZ" MOVES SOUTH

'There was a sudden and dramatic change when information was received that the "TIRPITZ" had left BOGENFJORD, although her destination was unknown. On 25.Oct.42 Admiral (Submarines) signalled "Carry out Operation Title. Target Tirpitz in FOETTENFJORD. Day D5 October 31st. Acknowledge. Wishing you all the best of luck."'

To describe the operation itself, there can be no better way than to look at the contemporary report prepared [held in the National Archives, Kew] by skipper Leif Larsen, just one month after *Arthur* set sail. Being carbon copy number six, and typed eighty years ago on flimsy paper, makes some of the place names difficult to decipher, in addition to which some of their spellings have changed during the intervening years. The names as discernible have been kept, followed by, so far as the author has been able to ascertain, the modern spelling in brackets. There is also a compass coordinate correction. At the latitude of 63°N, the difference of 1° in longitude would equate to a distance of around 31½ miles.

'MOST SECRET

'Copy No. 6.
'28th November 1942

'TITLE

'Report by Quartermaster Leif Larsen. K.K. D.S.M. R.N.N.
'References:
'Admiralty Charts Nos. 1972, 3105, 2306
'G.S.G.S. maps of Norway scale 1:100,000
'Nos. 47A, 47B, 47C, 47D, 50A, 50B

'Monday 26th October 1942

'I left Lunna Voe, Shetland at 12.14 in M/V 'ARTHUR'. My crew consisted of P.O. Bjørnøy, Engineer, R Strand, Wireless Operator and J Kalve, Assistant Engineer and Deckhand.

'I had as passengers
'Sub-Lieutenant Brewster   )
'AB [Able Seaman] Brown   ) No. 1. Chariot
'Sergeant Craig   )
'AB Evans   ) No. 2. Chariot
'AB Tebb   )
'AB Causer   ) Dressers

'I also had on board two operational chariots.

'I set a course to a position approximately 63°N, 4°30'E and I reached this position at 06.00 on Wednesday 28th October. There was an easterly wind for the first twenty-four hours of the passage, which backed and ended in a southerly direction. During the first twenty-four hours we averaged approximately three knots. The sea was very rough. Some of the British crew were seasick to begin with but they helped us all they could. I received great help indeed from Sub-Lieutenant Brewster. I took one watch with Kalve and Sub-Lieutenant Brewster took the other with either AB Tebb, AB Brown or AB Causer. It was a very happy party.

'At 06.00 on Wednesday 28th October we changed course to East by South and made landfall at Harøy [Harøya]. As we did not wish to arrive off the south end of Smølen [Smøla] before the first light on Thursday 29th October, we reduced speed. After sighting Harøy we changed course to Smøla and passed fifteen miles to the west of Grip light on the evening of Wednesday, 28th October. During the passage to Norway the chariots were held firmly by their lashings. The starboard chariot moved some inches but it was soon fastened. The ropes were tied tight enough but the blocks were not securely fastened but this was soon put right by nailing the blocks to the deck. The following is a timetable of the remainder of our journey which has been set out day by day.

'Thursday 29th October

'We passed north of Grip light and Lyngvaer [Lyngvær] and arrived at Hogoerne [Høgøyan] at 08.00 and anchored in the bay on the west side of Hogoerne 63°17'N, 7°58'E. There was an easterly wind which increased during the day. When we had had our breakfast we started work with the chariots. We unlashed them from the deck to charge them. To enable us to get at the charging motor we first had to take some of the peat out of the hold. We had some trouble in starting the motor. The exhaust pipe was leaking owing to the rough weather during the passage to Smøla. We charged one of the chariots for approximately 15 minutes and then the charging motor broke down. The holding down bolts on the motor had worked loose and the motor fell over and some parts of the engine were broken so it could not be used again. As it was impossible to repair those parts of the charging motor which were broken, Sub-Lieutenant Brewster decided not to try further to charge the chariots but to use them as they were.

'Before we started hoisting out the chariots and whilst they were still covered up, two fishermen came alongside and started talking to us. They were a bit suspicious as to what we had on deck and asked a lot of questions, particularly as to what kind of fishing we had had. After giving them a number of vague answers I asked them a lot of questions about the prohibited area 17 miles to the west of Smøla and I was told this area was patrolled by German planes and any fishing boats found in it were fired at. I then asked them why the area was prohibited and they told me that in the spring of 1942 there had been a boat from England which had landed some people there. The Germans had found out that a landing had been made in this area and had immediately declared the prohibited area. It is very hard to get away from Norwegians who talk.

'I could not find sheltered water which was sufficiently deep for hoisting out the chariots so as to allow them to hang Judas [Royal Navy slang for a rope insecurely made fast] to the full extent of the towing wires, so we sank them on a short piece of rope about 3 fathoms [18ft] deep. The water was very clear but it was the best place I could find for hoisting out the chariots.

'Shortly after we had sunk the chariots a fisherman came alongside in a rowing boat. He was alone and after looking around said, "What have you there." I replied, "Something for demolishing mines." He then said, "It looks like a U-boat." And I repeated, "Something for demolishing mines." He talked a bit with me and I asked him where he lived. He lived in Hogoerne in a hut by himself and I asked him if he wanted any butter or coffee. He took some from me. I told him that it was dangerous to talk and he replied, "Yes, I realise that." He then went away in his rowing boat. I am not quite sure what kind of a fellow he was but I think he was a loyal Norwegian. During the afternoon and evening there was an E.N.E. wind and it was later decided not to go to the Trondheim lead at 04.00 hrs. on Friday, 30th October, but to wait a little longer. During the day we saw two or three aircraft but they did not take any notice of us. We did not see any aircraft or patrol boats on the way from Shetland to Smøla.

'Friday 30th October

'At 04.00 the weather was just the same but during the day it improved and we started at 14.00 and decided to go to Hestviken [Hestvika, on the NE corner of the island of Hitra 63°34'N, 9°09'E] that evening. We towed the chariots on the short ropes until we reached deeper water when they were sunk on their normal towing wires and we proceeded at full speed. As soon as we had started at full speed we threw the charging motor and radio set and aerial overboard. We did not throw the guns overboard but took them below and put them in the hold. All the English food we had left, we also took into the hold. During this time the British crew were all below. We also arranged the peat so that the hold had the appearance of being full up to the hatches. As nothing was in sight in the Trondheim lead the British crew came on deck in the afternoon and remained on deck after dark. When we arrived at Hestvika we anchored in 10 fathoms to make sure that there was plenty of room for the chariots. The day before we arrived at Smøla the engine was going badly and during that afternoon and evening, the engine was getting worse and worse but we managed to get to Hestvika at 23.00 and dropped anchor there.

'I went to talk to Nils Strøm at Hestvika. Sorlie recommended him to me as a useful contact as he would be able to give me the latest information regarding the watchpost at Beian. His son directed me to a farmer who had a repair shop and I got some tools from him to repair the engine. The engine was in such a bad state that we would not be able to start it again. Before I went ashore to talk to Nils Strøm we took the engine to pieces. The cylinder was cracked at the top and then Bjørnøy, Strand, and Kalve worked all night with the engine and had it repaired at 07.00 the next morning (Saturday). The repairs were only temporary and would not have been sufficient to allow the M/V ARTHUR to put to sea but were just sufficient to allow her to proceed to the target area. We should not have been able to repair the engine without the tools we had managed to borrow. We borrowed a drill and a set of taps. We had plenty of tools with us but not the kind necessary to repair the engine. It was a good thing Bjørnøy was an excellent mechanic, otherwise the engine could not have been repaired.

'When I saw Strøm in the evening he gave us the following information regarding my passage through the controls. I should not show the *Fartsbok* [*sjøfartsboka*/logbook] but just show my *Tillåtelse til å fiske* [fishing permit] and would probably not be asked for any more papers. He said we would meet the examination boat after I passed Beian, somewhere between Beian and Agdenes [Agdeneståa]. Sometimes there is a patrol boat which is patrolling between Beian and a little into Trondheimsfjord and from Beian down to about 63°35'N and then back to Beian. He said it was quite easy to pass this boat. Strøm looked at my false papers and said he thought I had too many. I had been given some of the normal printed papers concerning the German regulations of not having any connection with England and describing the prohibited areas on the east. Strøm told me I need not produce these. I asked him if he knew anything of the movements of the target. He did not know it was here. I also asked him if he had seen any other warships or smaller ships. He told me that I would meet a watchboat before the minefield south of Garten. This watchboat patrols the fjord watching the minefield, and has nothing to do with the examination boat. It patrolled from the minefield to east of North Leksen [Nordleska]. It patrolled by night as well as day. Ships could also pass out of Trondheimsfjord by day and by night. He then said that I might meet some more watchboats close to Beian but the only boat I had to take any notice of was the examination boat.

'Strøm said the Norwegians would starve this winter. He had a grocer's shop but I could not see much stock. I asked him if I could have a pair of shoelaces and he said, "I have not seen such things for a long time." During the day we passed lots of merchant ships going north and south in Trondheim lead. These were not escorted or in convoy.

We could not see if there were any guns mounted on them. The ships were going up and down the fjord both by day and night.

'Saturday 31st October

'We started at 10.00. Our course was north of Storo [Stora] 63°33'N, 9°50'E and south of South Laksen [Sørleska] 63°34'N, 9°20'E and then east of Nordleska. We passed a patrol boat north of Laksen 100 yards away but no attention was paid to us. The patrol boat at Laksen had a cannon approximately the same size as our Oerlikon, probably between 20 and 40mm. I cannot remember for certain but I believe it was on the forecastle. The size of the ship was between 70 and 80ft. long. She was cruising at a slow speed using her engine only. We then proceeded up Trondheim, led to the north of the southern minefield, and past Garten and Beian. There were no patrol ships at Beian and we proceeded towards Agdeneståa. We had to keep to the northern side of Trondheim lead. We kept to the north side past Hovdeteson [Hovdetåa] 63°41'N, 9°39'E and then in a wide circle round Agdeneståa to the entrance of Trondheimsfjord where we met the examination boat. There was only one. She was in the middle of the fjord, due east of Agdeneståa. I saw two other boats passing the watchboat and noted what action they took. They went up to the examination boat and stayed there a little while and then proceeded towards Trondheim.

'When we slowed down just before approaching the examination vessel, I went on deck and Bjørnøy took over the wheel and the handling of the engine. Strand was on deck aft and Kalve was on deck with me. There was no peat on deck. When I reached the examination boat I went alongside and threw my rope on board which fastened us together. The examination boat just had weigh [*sic*] on and I came up slowly beside her. I did not have to go astern. I was then standing on the side of our boat and I waited for the Examination Officer to come on board. I took my *Tillåtelse til å fisks* and my consignment note out of my breast pocket and expected the officer to look at them, but he stood on board the ARTHUR and just looked around the deck and then headed straight for the after cabin. He went down into the cabin and sat down. I sat down too and handed over the *Tillåtelse til å fisks* pass only. He asked for the crew list and the *erlaubnisschein* [permit]. This time I did not show him the consignment note, the *Farsbok* or the *Merksbrev* [ship's registration papers]. The papers stating that no contact had been made with England were pinned to the crew list and the *erlaubnisschein*. He examined these carefully and was satisfied. He spoke very bad Norwegian. He remarked that he knew the German officer who had signed the *erlaubnisschein*. He said, "I know him from Bremen but I did not know he was in Aslesund." I had a quick look at the *erlaubnisschein* to see that it had the Aslesund [Aalesund/Ålesund] stamp on it.

'He glanced at the Crew List but did not peruse it carefully. He looked at the stamps on the reverse side of the Crew List to see where I had been and what controls I had reported to. He did not look at it carefully. Neither my, nor any of the crew's legitimate *jonskort* [ID card] were examined by the German Officer. He filled in a paper authorising "ARTHUR" to proceed down Trondheimsfjord to Trondheim. This paper had the stamp of the control at Hasselviken [Hasselvika]. As the stamp was marked Hasselvika Control, it would look as if Hasselvika is the place at which the examination vessel is based. The stamp was a plain oblong rubber stamp. The paper was coloured white and had on it the name and number of the boat. He did not fill in the length of the boat or the type of engine, although there was a space provided on the form. The only information he filled in was name, number, tonnage and cargo. I told him in Norwegian that the cargo was peat. I had to be careful not to use English words. He did not understand when I said "peat" in Norwegian, so I had to explain it was for burning in the fire, and that I was taking it into Trondheim. He then understood.

'He did not wish to know the name of the consignee but he wished to know where I came from. He asked me whether I had a radio or any photographic apparatus on board. He also asked if I had any passengers. To all these questions I answered no. He wished to know the number of the crew and I answered four which he inserted in the paper. He asked my name which he also inserted in the paper. There was a question on the paper "Is the crew controlled" and to this he inserted "Yes". The form was in German and Norwegian.

'There was also a question, "Have you got a *Erlaubnisschein*." He inserted "Yes" but did not ask for this again as he had already seen it. He then signed the paper. At the bottom there was a circular stamp with the German Eagle at the top, probably holding the Swastika in a circle. There was lettering around the outside of the circle of the stamp, but I do not remember what it was. The stamp was on the bottom left-hand corner. There was no stamp under his signature. He wrote his name and then his rank. I could not read his name but his rank looked as if it started with "Ober". By that time he was quite satisfied with my papers.

'When he examined the reverse side of the Crew List and noticed that I was registered at Eristisund he asked me if I liked the place. He seemed as if he would start a conversation, but I did not wish to give myself away by any means so in response to his question I just replied yes. He was down below for between ten minutes and quarter of an hour. He then came on deck, stopped at the engine room, and looked down there and right into the wheelhouse, but did not go in there at all. He looked in the forecastle but did not go in. He then went on board his own ship.

'There was another boat astern waiting so we went forward to allow the other boat to come up. I was scared that the German Officer would look down and see the chariots as the water was very clear. The examination vessel was approximately 60ft. long a Norwegian fishing cutter with a German Naval crew. I saw three Germans on deck and there was probably one German in the wheelhouse. I believe she had a gun but I was not certain. I did not notice the German boat very much as all my attention was on the German Officer and I was worried that he would look down and see the chariots. As far as I could see she had no wireless. The crew were not armed but the Officer had a pistol. When we passed Beian we saw many big bombers flying in and out of the fjord and circling in the fjord. They flew at a very low height and were of different types. After we had passed Beian until we were approximately off Lansviken [Lensvik] 63°31'N, 9°49'E we saw many aircraft patrols until it was dark.

'We left the examination boat and proceeded down Trondheimsfjord, we were not nervous about the chariots. They should have been quite all right as we had had fine weather all the way. We were not nervous that they would hit each other. We were all in very good spirits thinking the worst of the job had been done. The sea was calm and the weather was fine. At this time we were sheltered by the hills between Hassalvika and Strømsmag [Strømmen]. There is a valley leading down to Strømmen and as I reached the entrance to the valley I realised the wind might prove troublesome. We were sailing down just to the east of the centre of Trondheimsfjord.

'Just past Strømmen we met a small German warship which had two aeroplanes on deck merely for the purpose of transport. It was too small for a cruiser but was probably a destroyer. The British were at this time on deck but took shelter in the wheelhouse. The British came on deck as much as possible but took shelter directly anything came too near. The warship passed us and when we were in the wash we slowed down so as not to damage the chariots. When we reached Lonsviken we saw a yachtboat but it was getting dark and it was impossible to obtain any details of her. We then rounded Rødberget 63°29'N, 10°44'E [correctly 9°59.5'E) leaving it on the port beam half a mile away. The time was between 17.45 and 18.00. Rødberget light was burning.

'I felt an easterly wind here but still did not think it would be too bad. About 15 minutes after passing Rødberget with the wind E.N.E. we suddenly ran into two fairly large waves. The boat pitched and we could feel a drag on the chariots and a second afterwards one of the chariots hit the propellers. It seemed as if when the boat rose on the first wave the chariot was taught [sic] at the end of the towing wire but when the boat went down into the trough the towing wire slackened and suddenly became taught [sic] again when the boat rose on the next wave. At one moment we could feel the drag on the chariots and a second afterwards one of the chariots hit the propellers. We proceeded at slow speed to Frosta Tanges [Tangen, on the Frosta peninsula]. One of the divers, AB Evans, made ready to put on his diving suit to go out and to see if the second chariot was still there. I told Sub-Lieutenant Brewster that I did not think it safe for AB Evans to dive so we proceeded further intending to go up to Tangen and have a look when we came into the lee of the shore. I was quite certain the chariots had disappeared as I could feel it by the movement of the boat.

'As we proceeded up the Fjord we had a conference, I, Sub-Lieutenant Brewster and Sergeant Craig, as to what we should do if there was nothing left at all when the diver had been down. We then considered the chances of getting ashore in the Hakik area and meeting the car. I then told them it would not be possible to land there because of the strong sea, and because we could not get ten into the dinghy and it would not be possible for five of us to go in two trips to the shore. We cancelled the attempt of going ashore there and decided to go further along Frosta in the hope that the weather would get better. We decided to try and find somewhere just before Fasneshaven. Owing to the weather we did not get up to Tangen. The reason for this was that even if we had gone there the sea was too rough for the chariots to be cast off, so we proceeded to the North of Tautra to Nelham. There we stayed for a while and AB Evans dived down and had a look to see if the chariots were still there. He found that the towing wires were still attached to the boat and at the end of the wires were the shackles. Attached to the shackles were still the extra lead weights they had put on to make certain that the chariots towed deep enough in the water.

'Although the seas were considerably calmer here AB Evans bumped his head badly on the bottom of the boat. I feel certain that the weather was too bad for AB Evans to have had a look shortly after we thought we had lost the chariots. During the last hour before we reached Malhus [Breivika] we threw the majority of the peat overboard and made holes above the water line in the boat ready to sink her. We packed up our haversacks with food. We took no clothes with us, only socks because we had only three rucksacks. We arrived at Malhus at 24.00. Kalve took the wheel while I discussed the question of landing and our escape with Sub-Lieutenant Brewster, Sergeant Craig and AB Tebb. When we did land I was not quite certain where we were. I thought we were further north in the Trondheimsfjord than in fact we were. I did not find out my mistake until the day after we landed.

'We decided to land together and split up later. We lowered the rowing boat and five men went ashore, Kalve rowing, Sergeant Craig, AB Evans, AB Causer and Strand. Kalve had a very bad landing and came back with the boat half-filled with water. When he came back we took the ARTHUR half a mile further down the fjord. We had already made four or five holes in the side of the ship above the waterline and we had to keep the pump going to keep the water down. We then opened both sea cocks and the water flooded the engine room, stopping the engine of its own accord. The wind was blowing approximately N.E. and the boat should have drifted well west of Tautra into the middle of the fjord. Several hours should have passed from the time we left her before she finally sank.

'The remainder of the crew left the boat and took to the rowing boat. I was the last to leave the ARTHUR. We joined the other party on the beach at Melhust [*sic*] at 02.00 Sunday morning. All members of the party both Norwegian and British had a pistol. We left all the diving gear in the cabin which had been made in the hold of ARTHUR and the machine gun and all the weapons and ammunition. It was very heavy and to make certain the boat would sink we left everything in the hold. I took all the ship's papers with me but I believe I left on board my legitimate *jonskort*. The tow ropes were not detached from the boat as this was too big a job. There was some English food left aboard. We put this in the cabin in the hold.'

To some extent, it was surprising the party had made it so far as they did, as evidenced by Quartermaster R. Strand's report dated 7 December 1942, extracts from which follow:

'The engine started to go wrong on Tuesday 27th October, the day before we made landfall. The engine stopped twice while we were at sea. The first time we worked on the engine for one and a half hours until we were able to start it, but the second time it started easily. We had just started work on the hoisting out of the chariots when two fishermen came alongside in a small boat but they did not see the chariots as they had not been uncovered. We gave them some butter and told them not to talk. I heard that the charging motor had broken down but at the time I was cooking. It was impossible to repair.

'On Friday 30th October we went up Edøyfjord into Trondheim lead and then anchored on the north-east corner of Hitra having thrown the wireless set, aerial and generator overboard just after we started. The engine stopped just before we anchored and it was in such a bad state that we could neither go on or go back to England.

'The whole of the night Bjørnøy, Kalve and I worked on the engine. Bjørnøy did an excellent job of work. I thought it was impossible to do anything with the engine with such a bad set of tools. There were two holes in the middle of the head of the piston. We obtained some tools and some steel screws from the shore. We drilled holes in the piston larger than the holes we found and inserted the screws. We had to break the taps to sharpen them. We wondered if we should ever get *Arthur* to move but the engine started straight away.'

Prior to the scuttling of *Arthur*, Bob Evans had been sent down again to find out exactly what had happened to the chariots. He reported that the wire cables and hooks attaching them to *Arthur* remained intact, but that the warheads to which they were joined had torn themselves free: the eye bolts were still connected to strips of metal that had previously encased the shell of the warheads. Writing of these events years later, Commander Fell reflected that he still groaned whenever he thought of what these young men must have felt, when the full significance of the disaster dawned upon them: 'There they were, within one mile of their launching point, and only four miles from the world's most powerful battleship, with victory in their grasp. I feel certain that nothing could have stopped them wreaking such destruction to *Tirpitz* that even if she stayed afloat she could never have fought again.'

There was no room in Larsen's official report to mention his thoughts and feelings at that stage, nor those of the others in the party. Later, Sub Lieutenant Brewster was to say:

'We were dismayed. The chariots were gone and the attempt was off. I don't think anyone has ever been so disappointed as we were that night. We were ten miles from the pride of the German fleet; all our obstacles were behind us; and we might as well have been at the North Pole. Looking back, I don't remember one single curse. We were all too unhappy for that.'

For Larsen, Brewster and company, there could be no time for reflecting on what might have been: their efforts must now be wholly concentrated on the task of crossing German-occupied Norway on foot, heading for neutral Sweden and freedom.

Chapter 9

Escape to Sweden and Home.
Brewster's Party

After coming ashore from the now-scuttled *Arthur* at around 2.00 am on Sunday, 1 November 1942, the whole party headed inland for a while before splitting into two groups, with Larsen leading his party of four – Craig, Tebb, Evans and Kalve. They hoped to keep separate from the other party, giving each the best chance of avoiding unwanted attention. Brewster had in his party Causer, Brown, Bjørnøy, and Strand. Each party thus had two Norwegian nationals, able to speak with any locals they might meet and having knowledge of the country to be crossed.

Strand recalled:

'We all walked together to Bergsholden 445564 where we separated. Sub-Lieutenant Brewster took charge of our party to begin with but Bjørnøy and I had to take over as we knew the language. I was not very fit when we started our trip to Norway but I had been well trained and after two days I was quite all right. From Bergsholden we went north and walked to the north side of Hjeffassen 460540. We then walked due east just north of the Naval station at Flvik 483543. We then went north east over the mountains.'

In the extracts that follow, Brewster recounted their journey on foot to Sweden:

'We carried on through the rest of the afternoon and evening, not allowing ourselves any organised breaks for food. That night we forced a fishing hut and had some much needed sleep. We were all pretty weary and I suppose we took very few precautions. The nature of the whole business was such that it would have been impossible not to leave something to chance. We preferred to put speed before everything else, even at the cost of running some rather unwise risks during the daylight hours.

'We set off early the following morning and had a completely uneventful day. The weather was grand had been since the storm had gone down less than an hour after we had lost the machines. Malcolm Causer was beginning to feel the cold, but he never complained. We had a certain amount of warm clothing sweaters etc. but we really could have done with more. By nightfall we reckoned we were half-way across Norway. This meant we had covered twenty to thirty miles in the two days.'

Unable to find anywhere to rest up that night, they kept on walking through the darkness, due east by their compass. At daybreak on Tuesday, 2 November, they found a barn at the rear of a small farmhouse and were able to catch up on some sleep before later creeping away unseen. Contact with local inhabitants carried a double danger, that these people might reveal the party's whereabouts to the German occupying forces or that the latter might carry out reprisals against any locals deemed to be helping the 'enemy'. In spite of the danger, and as there was no sign of the Germans, Brewster decided to approach one of the isolated farms, having decided they deserved a comfortable night's sleep and some proper, hot food:

'We kept a likely looking farm under observation until nightfall. I then sent Bjørnøy and Kalve down to see what they could find out. We had our rucksacks and our route planned in case we had to do a quick bunk. But fortunately there was no need. Kalve came to find us and led us down. We had a wonderful meal of soup, eggs and potatoes, and were then taken up to the loft. The hay was divinely comfortable and we slept soundly with someone else to do the worrying for us. Our hosts father, mother and two grown-up sons were just grand. 'Entertaining' us would have meant facing a firing squad if a German patrol had chanced to find us there. But they didn't seem to be worried.'

At three o'clock the next morning, Wednesday, 3 November, Brewster and company, each having been provided with a packed lunch, set off, escorted by the farmer's two sons. The boys guided the party throughout the morning until they stopped for a midday meal break in a little hillside hut overlooking a valley.

'Soon after we restarted we got to the top of this range, and they showed us a jagged line of mountain peaks which marked the Norwegian–Swedish border. This done, they turned, gave us a brief good-bye and set off back down into the valley. They left themselves precious little time to get back to the farm before dark. I have no idea who these people were, but the physical and mental help they were to provide us enabled us to carry on our trek, feeling on top of the world.'

The going was becoming more challenging as by now the terrain was steep and hilly with no shelter, heavy snowdrifts adding to their difficulties. Exhausted, frozen and with blistered and sore feet, they were grateful to find an empty shooting lodge where, after forcing an entry, they managed to light a fire. They were even able to make flapjacks with some flour and rancid butter they found there.

'On the seventh morning we tidied up the place and went on up, getting a bit excited and saying sweet things about the snow, very deep now. By early afternoon we reached the last barrier, a range of mountains 6,000 feet high. We carried on and reached Sweden early on the eighth morning after a trying night. There was glare on the snow, and we were suffering not only from frostbite, but from snow blindness, and kept falling over rock faces and into snowdrifts. With the help of Benzedrine we eventually came to a small Swedish village and gave ourselves up, pretty dishevelled, unshaven for ten days, hungry, but apart from Causer, we were otherwise all right. Malcolm was in a bad way. He had been in pretty bad pain for the last couple of days, but had said nothing about it. It was frost-bite, of course. He was obviously the most susceptible, coming from Brazil, but it is a wonder Brown and I weren't troubled too. The local police were very friendly, and before any sort of interview could get under way we asked them to send for a doctor to look at Malcolm's feet. The doctor was most concerned. Not long after this Malcolm was separated from us and, as we learnt when he eventually rejoined us in Scotland, was packed off to a Swedish hospital, where he spent a very pleasant month.'

The police chief, not seemingly very concerned with this party of strangers, asked: 'Who are you and how did you get here?' They replied: 'We are Norwegian and British Servicemen and we walked across Norway.' He then informed them that another party had arrived that morning with the same story. It was, of course, Larsen's party.

Chapter 10

Escape to Sweden and Home. Larsen's Party

'der lyset ikke er skilt fra mørket, der ingen grenser et satt,
bare en stillhet.' (Gunvor Hofmo, 1948)
Trans. 'where the light is not separated from the
darkness, where no boundaries are set, only a silence.'

The two escape reception parties, organized by Odd Sørli and his associates of the Lark resistance movement, waited in vain for the arrival at the rendezvous of the men they were to whisk across Norway by car to the safety of Sweden. Their non-appearance at and beyond the expected time could only mean that the men had met with problems. The absence of loud explosions from the direction of Fættenfjord also served to confirm the failure of the mission. Having no means of communicating with the escapees, the reception parties held on for as long as they dared, then dispersed before their presence, in what was a sensitive military area, attracted the attention of the German patrols.

Using a large-scale map of Norway and a facility available via the internet, 'Norgeskart', the author has endeavoured, with difficulty and little measure of success, to follow the subsequent route of escape as described in Larsen's report. Norwegian historian and lecturer Frode Lindgjerdet, author of the book *Opersajon Title*, written in his native tongue, explains:

'As the reports gives map coordinates, I had to use the same maps to locate where they went and use my military experience to deduce their avenues of advance. This was especially difficult on land. Several place names have since changed, or they were misspelt in the reports. On several instances they were simply lost. Despite being experienced navigators and mariners, they were poor orienteers. On one occasion they claimed to have gone north when they clearly ended up south of their previous position. This can easily happen if you hold your compass 180 degrees wrong, a common mistake that you probably are not aware of if you are used to compasses fixed on a ship. I also travelled parts of the route when things did not make any sense, or conferred with people I knew had local knowledge of the areas. Sometimes I was completely lost until the descriptions suddenly made sense.'

The author of this book, figuratively taking a leaf out of Frode Lindgjerdet's book, also made enquiries of people with local knowledge of the place names mentioned. A particular problem was trying to identify on a map the place name 'Melhus'. Larsen gives this as his landing place on the Frosta peninsula after having scuttled *Arthur* north of the island of Tautra. In respect of my quest, two people responded most helpfully to enquiries. Firstly, Magne K. Christiansen of the Butikksjef Extra Frosta Coop supermarket, who advised me that Melhus is not a place name but a family name, the family living not far from Breivika, where the boat went ashore. Then came a message from Jorunn Sterten Melhus, a local folk musician and teacher living in the village of Frosta, who told me her surname comes from her husband's family from Inderøya, a peninsula more to the north in the Trondheimsfjord. She explained that Melhus means 'between houses/homes', or 'the farm in the middle'.

Larsen's report dated 28 November 1942 continues the story of his party's escape:

'Sunday, 1st November

'After we landed at Melhus [Breivika] we all walked together up to a nearby road where we had some food. We continued walking approximately eastwards but as we were walking through woods and around farms, we could not keep a good direction. We saw nobody during the morning. We walked until approximately 06.00. We slept in the woods until 08.00. Nobody kept guard. We continued again at 08.00 until we came to the side of a lake. We had decided to split up shortly after we started that morning. We split up as follows;

'Sergeant Craig, AB Tebb, AB Evans and Kalve and myself in one party, and Sub-Lieutenant Brewster, AB Causer, AB Brown, Strand and Bjornøry in the other. My party went south and the other north. My party continued across country and not along the road. Sergeant Craig and I both had compasses. We were steering by compass south west of the lake. We ate some chocolate but did not stop for breakfast. We had plenty of chocolate.

'Very soon after we split up into two parties we came to a lot of farms and open country. It would have been too far to make use of what wood there was for cover so we went across country in two parties, Kalve and Sergeant Craig and myself in one and AB Evans and AB Tebb in the other. After we reached the top of a small hill we waited for Evans and Tebb to join us, then we all sat down and had a good meal.

'We continued over the hillside and saw lying in Lofjord a German battleship. I could see we were in the neighbourhood due east of Deleve [Dalsveet]. The time was 14.00. We passed a house 100 yards away and there were some people outside the house. We then proceeded north eastwards through the woods towards Hanebo [Hånnåbogen]. We had very great difficulty going round the farms and lakes which we met and it was impossible to know exactly where we were. We continued until we were south west of Hoglimpen [Høgklimpen] 550570. We found a barn containing hay. The farm was about 200 yards away but we did not go to it. This was in the evening about 08.00. We lifted the door off the barn, had a good meal there and went to sleep in the barn. At that time we were very tired indeed and we all slept very well that night. I woke up early the next morning (Monday) because it was so cold and draughty.

'**Monday, 2nd November**

'We had breakfast in the barn at daylight. There was nobody about. The farmhouse lay up on the hill in the wood and we could not actually see the house from the barn. We did not know precisely where we were, so we decided to go up to the house. The Englishmen went past it. I and Kalve went up to the house intending to ask where we were, but the house was empty. We kept on walking but our direction was very much north east as we encountered great difficulties wide open spaces, lots of farms and very little cover.

'We started about 09.00 and we kept walking all that day until that evening about 18.00 we passed Ronglan station 621602. We crossed the railway leading from Levanger to Trondheim. After we had passed the railway we went on the road going northwards for about 10 minutes. As there were a number of houses there, we left the road and headed eastwards up a small hill. There were plenty of small houses around here and we looked for another barn where we could again sleep. The time was approximately 19.00.

'We did not find anything satisfactory so we kept on looking around the barns until around 20.00. We then found a house standing by itself on the side of a wood. We decided to go in and talk to the people. I and Kalve went in for a talk with them and to ask them if we could make a meal by ourselves in the kitchen so that we could get something warm.

'We talked to the farmer who asked us in. He enquired whether we had any food and I told him we had food but wanted somewhere to heat it up. Then I told him we had some people outside and that they were Englishmen, and I told him the story that we had met them out on the coast and we were going to help them to the border. I said they were airmen who had fallen down, as I knew there had been English planes over the Trondheim area on Sunday.

'We went in and his wife made coffee for us and gave us some biscuits. She also gave us some bread. They were very nice people. I cannot tell whether they knew we had come from England. We did not tell them but I feel certain they realised it. Before the farmer asked us in he said, "You know how it is, if the Germans knew we had taken in anybody here." I replied, "Yes, but we do not know you and you do not know us and we do not know where we are, so that when we leave early in the morning, nobody will be any the wiser." He seemed perfectly satisfied and it was quite all right because I did not know where we were.

'We had a very comfortable evening with the farmer, sitting round the table in the kitchen. We got very warm and comfortable. We did not wash. We were so sleepy and tired and all we thought of was going to bed so that we could get off early in the morning. We asked the farmer about sleeping in the barn, and then he said it was better to sleep in the cow house. There were plenty of cows there and this made it very warm. He came and called us at 05.00 the next morning. The house where we spent the night was somewhere near Skjekemp [Skjele].

'Tuesday, 3rd November

'We were called by the farmer at 05.00. We went into his kitchen again and had some coffee and food. He gave us some bread and some good cakes. They were very nice to us. We left this farmhouse at 06.00.

'Soon after we left the barn we buried our papers in a wood beside the track. There was no snow here so nobody could follow our tracks and find them. We went on to a minor road leading north east from Ronglan running parallel and to the east of the main road. We were forced further north than we intended as we could not turn eastward because of all the farms in the area. Sometime about 09.00 we reached the main road to the south west of Skjerve and crossed it in a northerly direction and then reached the railway again.

'We saw there were so many small farms on the way we wished to take that we could not pass them in the daytime as there were insufficient woods for us to travel through. We therefore hid in a small wood the whole day between the main road and the railway. We had a meal at midday and started off again at 17.30. We went on to the main road and walked north east to Skjerve and then on the minor road going south west to Røysing. We followed the minor road eastward to Markabygd [Markabygda]. We went through the village to the end of the road until we got to the furthermost farm at Tretten.

'About 21.00 in the evening we went in and talked with the farmer, telling him the same story we had told the people in the farm at Skjerve. We stayed there for the night. We had a good meal that evening in the farm itself and we also got a bed in the house. We had a good breakfast the next morning. On the roads that day we met some people with horses and wagons. I and Kalve walked first and the three Englishmen followed behind. We walked past these people without exchanging greetings.

'Wednesday 4th November

'We had breakfast at the farm at Tretten. We used our own food as we had enough for our own use although we had to ration it later. They gave us porridge for breakfast, milk and eggs. We took our uncooked eggs with us. Kalve and I left our pistols with one of the sons of the owner of the farm.

'We started off again about 08.00. By this time we had reached the beginning of the hills and the going was very rough. A couple of hours after we had left Tretten we came into the snow on the hills. One of the sons came with us as far as Ensrakallen [Kaarskallen] on our journey to show us the way. We walked eastward all day until we came to a hut on the west side of Haugevola [Haugsvola]. We arrived there about 15.00. We did not meet anybody on the way. We did not go any further because we were not sure whether we would be able to find any more huts before darkness fell.

'The hut we found in the hills was one the farmers used in summertime. We had to break into the hut. There were bunks, blankets, mattresses and cooking utensils. There was no food except a tin of tea which we took. There was plenty of wood in the kitchen for a fire and we had a fire going all night. We cooked ourselves a hot meal and went to sleep.

'Thursday 5th November

'We got up and cooked our eggs and had a hot breakfast. We cleared up the hut as well as we could and jammed the door. We had had to break the lock to get into the hut, so we put a stick in front of the door so as to stop it banging.

'We left at 09.45 and later passed south of Grønningen lake and then passed north of Hermosanasen [Hermannssnasa]. From there we went to Tvervola [Tverrvola]. We had intended to walk from Tverrvola to the north side of Eraskfjeld [Kråkfjellet?] that night but we had just passed the top of Tverrvola when it started to get dark. We saw some farms in a north easterly direction and decided to go there. When looking at the map I thought the farms were a good deal south of the road from Levanger to Sweden but on approaching them I found that the farms were very close to the road.

'We then went to the first farm at Brenan [Brenna] approximately 14 kilometres from the border, intending to tell the same story as before and to try to get somewhere to sleep. Kalve and I went to the house while the Englishmen stayed outside. It was now between 17.45 and 18.30. The farmer told us we could not stay in his farm because he did not have any hay, but he pointed to another farm and said that the people there used to take in tourists. At the same time he told us that at the end of the road on the border there were Germans and he also told us there were two State policemen in the village but they were living high up on the hill, far to the north of the road. We then went to what we thought was the second farm but by a mistake we went to the wrong one. We were told that the third farm we came to would be the one which took tourists. When we came to the third farm they told us they did not take tourists but there should be a house further along the road. By this time we were a bit suspicious so we went along the road discussing what we should do and I thought it might be wise not to stop there.

'We then came to a turn in the road and just past this bend we met two policemen. It was about 19.15. It was very dark so we did not see them right away but we could tell they were policemen. Sergeant Craig and I were in front and the others were just behind. When they were near us I saw one was in uniform and had a German automatic rifle in his hand. The other one was in civilian clothes. I could not see if he had a pistol, but he was pointing at us with his hand. He may have been holding something. They ordered us to stop. They were then three or four feet away. I am not sure whether the people in the village warned the policemen or not. The man at the first farm we came to might have warned them but on the other hand he told us about the Germans at the border and the policemen. However, if the police were stationed to protect the road they would not have been on the hill to the north of the village but would have been patrolling the road.

'The policeman in civilian clothes told us to walk along and I asked where we had to walk to. "You just walk," he said, pointing in the direction we had been going. We didn't go so he ordered us to drop our sticks which we did, and then the man in civilian clothes asked the man in uniform if he had his safety catch off and he replied "Yes". He was pointing the gun at me. We were then ordered to go along again and I asked where he wanted us to go. He then said, "You just go or we shoot." After this he ordered us to put our hands up.

'The man in civilian clothes was talking with an Oslo dialect, I think the man in uniform was German. He did not speak but he must have understood Norwegian as he answered "yes" in the right places when we were told to put our hands up. I lifted my hands as there was nothing more to argue about. We were again told to walk along. I told Sergeant Craig to draw his pistol and have it ready but he did not get it out quick enough. At the time we were told to put our hands up AB Tebb had his pistol in his hand. Kalve told Tebb to shoot and Tebb started shooting.

He fired three shots. I did not see this as I was in front but this is what Tebb told me afterwards. Tebb fired two shots at the man in civilian clothes and one at the man in uniform. The man in uniform started firing. After three shots Tebb's gun jammed and he could not fire any more. The policeman in uniform finally fired three more shots in between us.

'Then everybody started to run. There was a fence just beside the road. Some of us started to jump over it. Tebb and I ran down the road a little further, jumped over the fence into a field, crossed the field and managed to reach the river in a southerly direction. All firing had ceased and everything was quiet. We managed to meet Sergeant Craig down by the river. I asked if he had seen Kalve and was told that Kalve had just kept along the river going eastwards. I then asked about AB Evans and he said that AB Evans was lying in the road, either wounded or killed by the policeman.

'I was too far in front to see what had happened to AB Evans. Everything had happened so quickly that it was all over before we had had time to think. We decided to go along the river and cross it, so we started going eastwards but as it was very hard going there we went up on to the road again. By this time we had seen no sign of Kalve. I looked for his tracks but could not see them. It was much too dark to see anything. I was hoping we would catch up with Kalve but we did not do so. We discussed whether we should go back and see if we could find Evans but if he had been wounded or killed we would not have been able to do anything for him. At the time we came through the last village Evans had very bad feet and he could not walk much more that day. If he had been wounded he would not have been able to walk at all.

'We walked along the road for about an hour. I reckoned that one of the policemen would go and 'phone the Germans at the border, in which case we might meet a German car on the road when we went along. I told Sergeant Craig and AB Tebb to keep a good look out in front in case anybody came out on us. After about 20 minutes we saw the headlights of a car coming. We jumped off the road and hid behind some trees. We then saw it was not a car but a motor-bike. We could not see who was on it or if it had a sidecar attached as the headlights were too strong. After that had passed we went up on the road again and went on walking until 20.20 when we came to a bridge over the river. At this point the road and the river were very close. After we had crossed the river we went up on to the hillside. We stopped and had some food and looked at the maps. We then decided to go in a south easterly direction to get on to the Carl Johan Road. We reached the road and kept on it all the way until we reached the border the next morning at 02.15.

'Some eight miles from the border we saw two ski tracks but we knew there had been two Norwegians passing there the week before on their way to Sweden. When we were at Tretten we had been told that the Norwegians had left for the border so we knew to whom these tracks belonged.

'Friday 6th November

'We crossed the border at 02.15 and arrived at Skelstuen [Skalstugan] at 05.00. The place where we crossed was marked with boundary stone No 164. One side of the road is marked in Norwegian and on the other side is Swedish. We knew there could be no Germans there because there were no tracks and to have come round from the northern road they would have had to climb the mountains. There is a German patrol at Sandviken [Sandvika] on the border. I learnt afterwards that Kalve did not cross the river but crossed the road again in a northerly direction and passed north of Ingerhalmen.

'We were on the road to Skalstugan for two hours. We cleared our pockets of everything that had any marks on it, including our identity discs. AB Tebb threw his gun away. After the shooting Sergeant Craig had given his gun to Kalve, so that our party had one gun and Kalve had one. When we had thrown everything away we went into a military camp.

'We passed the tank barrier. The guard was in the guardroom and we walked right in before he saw us. The guard was very anxious that we should not tell the officer that we had walked into the camp without being seen. We had to wait as it was early and there was nobody about. The guard was quite nice to us. There was myself, Sergeant Craig and AB Tebb. When we came over the border we should have separated but nobody liked to go off the road and go somewhere else as we might have got lost. We thought it best to keep together and the story I was going to tell was that the two Englishmen had been shipwrecked and that I met them in the mountains as they were trying to get over the border and as I was also going to Sweden, I walked along with them.

'AB Tebb made some tea on the stove in the guard room and the guards helped us. They were quite friendly. We were very tired and sleepy. We had taken Benzedrine tablets just before starting over the border.

'After breakfast we were taken to the officer of the camp and he questioned us. He had one interpreter for the Englishmen and I told my story in Norwegian. I told him that I came from Elms near Levanger and he asked me why I had left there for Sweden. I said that I had received a telephone call from a friend in Trondheim that I should go to Sweden and that I should clear out of the district because I had been doing some work in connection with some propaganda and I had been working with an illegal paper in Trondheim. The officer was quite satisfied with this story, but how much he believed I do not know. He did not ask us very much more.

'Later in the day the officer called me and asked if I had passed through Verdal and I replied that I had not but had been across the mountains. He asked me where we had come onto the Carl Johan Road and I said that we came on to this road after we had got into Sweden. Then he told us that the Germans had telephoned that if anyone came into Sweden they should be chased back again, because the Germans were expecting someone to go over, but he did not know anything about the shooting. I think he believed us when I said we had come across the mountains. They found out afterwards that we had come along the Carl Johan Road because they found our tracks. The Customs officer told me they knew which way we had come. They were all very friendly to us and did not ask too much. At 11.00 Sergeant Craig and AB Tebb were sent away but I do not know where they went to.

'Saturday 7th November

'I left Skalstugan at 08.00. A Customs officer came on the bus with me to the railway station. I do not remember the name of the station but it was on the Storfliss Railway. From there I went to Matmar on the train. I went alone as the Customs officer left me at the station. I went straight to the Matmar Hotel as I had been told to report there, and arrived at 15.00. Kalve arrived the next day [Sunday] at around the same time. I stayed there that night and Sunday, and was treated very well.

'We were not supposed to go out of the Hotel, but as they were not very strict we did go to the village and bought some chocolate. We also managed to get some cigarettes. When Kalve arrived he had a policeman with him. I spoke to him.

'Monday 9th November

'Kalve and I left by train for Kaasanther. On the train we met Sub-Lieutenant Brewster, Sergeant Craig, AB Tebb and AB Brown. They came up and spoke to us. I suppose we should not have spoken to them but we did. We had no escort.

'Tuesday 10th November

'We arrived at Kassanther [Keæsather] at 03.00.

'During the next three days I had to complete all the various formalities and answer the usual questions that were put to me. I had a hard time to explain what I had been doing since I left school until the time I got into Sweden. I do not think that my questioner realised that I had come from England.

'I went to see the Manager of the camp and asked his permission to go to Stockholm to see somebody. As he would not let me go until I told him who I wanted to go and see, I told him it was Captain Hendriksen, the Norwegian Naval Attaché. He then looked at me and asked if I had come from England and I replied that I had. He said that I could not go to Stockholm the next day as he could not arrange things as quickly as that but he would do his best for me, so I just had to wait.

'Wednesday 11th November

'The next day Kalve was sent for by Mr Torsen. Mr Torsen makes a record of all complaints or charges made by people who have just come from Norway. Torsen knew some people who came from the same place as Kalve. I told Kalve that if he were asked questions about which he did not know what to answer he should come to me. Torsen asked him if he had come from England. Kalve said 'No, but I have a friend of mine here. Would you like to talk to him?' He then came for me and Torsen again asked Kalve if he had come from England and Kalve replied that he had.

'Torsen was a helpful fellow and I found him quite all right. I told him that I had come from England and was wanting to see somebody in Stockholm.

'Thursday 12th November

'We spent Thursday in the camp. As soon as anybody had finished with their part of the examination and we were standing idly in the camp, somebody got hold of us and made us work. We had to dig and carry things to the kitchen and the like. Strand arrived at the camp and we talked to him. He was in good spirits.

'Friday 13th November

'During my examination by another policeman, he checked my story with his criminal records as he mixed me up with another man of the same name.

'Saturday 14th November

'I went to Stockholm at about 14.00 with Kalve and we arrived there at 17.30. I was told at the camp by one of the officials at Keæsather that there would be a woman to meet us at the station at Stockholm. This woman took us to a small hotel where we stayed and I went up to the office on Monday 16th November.

'Mr Scappel had been looking for us at the station but had not seen us. I went to see Mr Scappel on Monday morning and he took me along to Mr Nielsen of the British Legation and I told Mr Nielsen the story. I was ready to fly that night but the aircraft did not go. I started to fly to England on Wednesday but the plane had to return.

'Thursday 19th November

'We finally flew from Stockholm.

'Friday 20th November

'We arrived at Leuchars airport at 08.00. I was not searched at all.

'Saturday 21st November

'I arrived in London this morning.'

So ended Larsen's report. After reading it, Admiral Sir Henry Ruthven Moore, vice chief of the Naval Staff, sent the following message to the participants of Operation Title:

> 'Although we know that through ill-luck the very gallant efforts to carry out the operation failed to achieve their object, I should like – on behalf of Flag Officer (Submarines) and of the Naval Staff – to express to you our admiration and deep appreciation of the vital part played by SOE and particularly by the Norwegian Section. Without their cooperation and valuable assistance the operation could never have been undertaken and I should like to ask you to convey our grateful thanks to all those concerned. Better luck next time!'

History does not record the thoughts of the Brazilian-born Malcolm Causer or Palmer Børnjøy upon learning of Admiral Moore's words. They spent some considerable time in hospital in Sweden receiving treatment for their frostbitten feet. As late as mid-March 1943, almost five months after arriving in Sweden, Bjørnøy was still in hospital, minus several toes.

It is obvious from Larsen's report concerning the shooting incident that confusion reigned, and that in the dark it was difficult for a clear picture of the actual sequence of events to be gained. It was very much a case of each man for himself. For another take on events surrounding this affair, we can do no better than look at Billy Tebb's report. It was he, after all, who had fired the shots:

'I, Leslie William TEBB, A.B. D/JX.145550 of 19 Sidebotham Street, BENDBURY [*sic* – Bredbury] STOCKPORT, in the County of CHESTER make oath and say as follows:

'1.   I joined the Royal Navy on August 12th 1935, and volunteered for special service in April 1942. I was drafted to the 12th Submarine Flotilla shortly afterwards.

'2.   During the month of October, 1942, I was ordered to take part in an attack on the German battleship TIRPITZ under the command of Lieutenant W.R. Brewster, R.N.V.R.

'3.   Owing to defects and bad weather the attack on the TIRPITZ was abandoned and the party landed in Norwegian territory with the intention of escaping to Sweden. We were divided into two parties, one in charge of Lieutenant Brewster and the other of a Norwegian called LARSEN, a quartermaster in the Royal Norwegian Navy. The other members of LARSEN'S party were Sergeant DONALD CRAIG, A.B. ROBERT P. EVANS and another Norwegian. For the first three days we marched, mainly by day, along the road towards the Norwegian frontier and laid up at night. On the fourth day we laid up during the day, and when dusk approached we decided to continue our march. We went on to the end of the road and got help from a house in the village there; they gave us food and a bed for the night. We left the village in the morning and marched across the mountain all that day: our hosts sent their son with us to guide us for part of the time. We spent the night at a shooting lodge belonging to a Quisling Norwegian and continued our march the next morning. We again marched all day and were approaching the Swedish frontier near SANDVIKEN: we called at a house after dark and asked for assistance which was refused: we then went back on to the road and again asked for help: we were given warm milk and continued our march.

'A few moments after, we were challenged on the road by two men who ordered us to put up our hands: one man had a revolver and a torch and the other an automatic weapon resembling a Sten gun. LARSEN spoke to the man and they asked him to accompany them to their picket house. LARSEN refused and they then threatened us with their weapons. After argument we all put up our hands and started marching towards the picket house. LARSEN, the other Norwegian and CRAIG were in front, EVANS and I came next and the two men with guns brought up the rear. I decided that our only hope of escape was for me to draw the revolver I was carrying under my left arm-pit and try to shoot our way out. I told the party this in English and EVANS assented to my proposal. I brought my right hand down, grabbed my revolver, turned and fired at the man immediately behind me. He was the man with the pistol and I hit him in the stomach: he fell but his companion opened fire with his automatic weapon. LARSEN and his party started running but EVANS did not move: he turned round to face the man who was firing and was shortly after hit and fell. I walked towards the man who was firing and shot at him: he fell down. I thought EVANS must be dead so I ran off to join the other members of the party. I caught up with LARSEN and eventually CRAIG and we made our way together across the frontier into SWEDEN.

'4.   So far as I can recollect EVANS was not wearing his good conduct badge which had been issued to him but he had on him his seaman's pay book and identity card which clearly showed that he was a member of the Royal Navy. Like me he was wearing a blue Gieves tropal suit.'

Tebb's report serves to highlight that self-preservation was the order of the day, especially given the fact that the frontier and freedom were so close. As Tebb thought that Evans was dead, he would have conveyed that thought to the other three in the party so it is perhaps surprising that Evans was later to be reported as 'Missing' rather than 'Killed in action'. On the other hand, as there was no proof positive that he was dead, then possibly this was the official line to be taken. In defence of Tebb and the others, their first duty, and no doubt their orders, were to escape. Had they gone back, they would have found Evans alive but unconscious, with a bullet wound to his thigh rather than his stomach. He has been described as about 6ft tall and very broad in the shoulders. Given these factors and his wound, it would have been impossible for the other four to carry him across the rocky, snow-covered terrain for the distance still to be covered to safety while avoiding capture by the now-alerted border police. If it did enter their mind that Evans was still alive, their conscience would be salved with the thought that the Germans would, upon finding him, tend his wound and treat him fairly as a prisoner of war under the terms of the Geneva Convention.

Another different version of this incident, thought to have been dictated by Larsen, was written in 1947 by Frithjof Saelen [see Notes 20] in his book *None But The Brave*:

'"Halt!"

'They had just turned a corner and two figures appeared in front of them as though by magic. The group was taken completely by surprise; they were still several miles from the frontier and had not expected to encounter any trouble. Worn out as they were after their struggle through the mountains, they had relaxed their watchfulness. Now they stood staring at two revolvers covering them, their pistols completely inaccessible in their back pockets. One of the two men confronting them had on grey-green German uniform with top boots and shoulder belt. The other was in navy blue civilian clothes or dark uniform, and his finger twitched on the trigger of his gun.

'"Where are you going?" he demanded sharply.

'"Who asks?" asked Larsen calmly, standing right in front of him. The German military policeman levelled the mouth of his revolver about a yard away from his head, obviously having no compunction about using it.

'"Shut up!" screamed the man in blue. "*I am asking you!* Drop your sticks!" His voice was shrill and quivered slightly; Larsen realised that he was just as frightened as the men from *Arthur.* Commando training and ju-jitsu flashed into his mind. For a moment he gathered his body, contracted his muscles and then leapt at the two men like an uncoiled spring, smashing them over backwards with the entire weight of his body. A second or two later a report went off behind him. Billy had got out his pistol, and the man in blue crumpled in a heap. But the German in uniform managed to fire wildly at them as he plunged off the side of the road. The rest of the group had drawn their pistols by now and shots followed the man down the slope. He disappeared into the darkness.

'Bob Evans lay on the ground. A bullet had torn his right calf badly. He was the only one who had been hit. The men examined him and Larsen realised that he would have to be left behind; there might be more Germans nearby and they had to get away as fast as possible, over the mountains now instead of through Sandvika.

'Evans was in uniform, and when they planned the attack back in England they reckoned that in such a case as this the British members of the party would be treated as prisoners of war. It was different for the Norwegians; they were dressed as civilians and could not risk being taken. There were hurried handshakes with the injured man and then they fled down to the Inna, which ran beside the road.'

While Saelen's account is somewhat in the style of a *Biggles* novel from the pen of Captain W.E. Johns, it confirms the essential facts: Evans had been shot and left to the mercy of the Germans. Ignoring Saelen's style, his vivid account of Larsen and company's trek across Norway puts flesh on the bones of the latter's skeletal report. Saelen tells us what conditions were like after landing from *Arthur*:

'It rained a cold, bitter rain, which the wind drove into their faces. The Englishmen were in battledress and the others in dungaree trousers and civilian jackets; they could not use their oilskins on the journey across country. Wind and rained combined to make life anything but cheerful. Through the hours of darkness they plodded along, sullen and obstinate. The high heather and bushes were heavy with rain and drenched them from the knees downwards. Their trouser legs became heavy and stiff with water and hit against each other at every step. Branches reached out at them in the darkness, scratching their faces, and slippery fallen leaves and rotten tree stumps caused them to fall headlong again and again. It was a miserable march.'

Describing conditions facing the party a day or so later, Saelen continues:

'The country on the way up the mountains was steep and heavy going, and the further up they struggled the more difficult it became. The snow was blown in huge drifts in the cracks in the rocks, and in some places they had to set their feet sideways to get a footing at all, while down in the hollows they paddled in snow up to their waists. The struggle soon began to tell on them, wearing them out and making their joints stiff. No amount of swearing helped, the only thing was to clench their teeth and get on as well they could. Sweat ran down them as they struggled upwards. If the snow was hard enough to bear them for a little way they could be sure that they would soon come to a place where they would sink straight through. Their bodies were wet with sweat and the snow seeped through their clothes, freezing them to the very bone.'

After a night in the scant shelter provided by a mountain hut (as described by Larsen's report for 4/5 November), Saelen gives his readers a verbal picture of the physical challenges presented by an off-road trek, ever upwards, through a Norwegian November:

'In order to get anywhere without every man being completely exhausted they had to organise how to clear the way. They made a line and then the first man went stamping and trampling down the snow for about ten yards, when he was replaced by the next man. It took a long time and was heavy work, and in some places the snow reached up to their waists. The men crept gradually upwards and onwards, fighting not to give up. At every step their strength flagged more. Each time they stopped for a rest it was more difficult to get up again, and after a while the pauses began to increase. As they ploughed on, progress became slower and slower. It was so good to sit down and lean back with your head in the snow and close your eyes. Then you did not feel the wind, nor the dreadful aching of your limbs. Your eyes shut of their own accord; sleep stood beckoning like a beautiful woman, like an angel who would shield you from the cold and the nightmare struggle. They had to shake themselves and tear themselves away from the temptation, drag themselves to their feet and go on again. On and on.'

It was Thursday, 5 November, and after a whole day struggling through the snow, according to Larsen's report, it was between 5.45 pm and 6.30 pm when they came across a farm. Although just less than 9 miles (14km) from the border with Sweden, the party needed rest and shelter for the night. They were turned away from three farms in an unfriendly and unhelpful fashion, which led Larsen to report: 'By this time we were a bit suspicious.' Rightly so, as events proved. In his book, Saelen elaborates on what occurred at the third farm with an account that must surely have come to him from Larsen himself:

'At the next farm they met a bad-tempered old woman. When she heard what they wanted she called them a lot of

The German battleship *Tirpitz* anchored in a Norwegian fjord

Tirpitz (The Beast) at sea

Shetland Bus Memorial (Courtesy Scalloway Museum)

Channel Island fortification (Operation Basalt) (Courtesy Société Jersiaise)

Two divers on a Chariot practice run in a Scottish loch

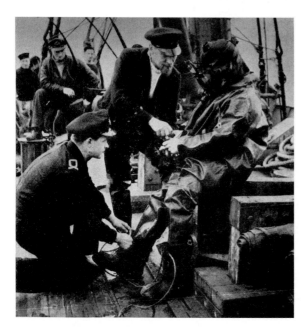

Dressing a diver into a 'Clammy Death' Sladen suit.

Loading and unloading a Chariot

King George VI inspecting divers

Arthur sailing up Trondheim Fjord towards Rødberget. Painting by Glyn L Evans

Arthur hits stormy seas. Painting by Edgar Hodges (Courtesy Scalloway Museum)

Grini Detention Centre, Oslo

Halifax bomber towing a Horsa glider (Operation Freshman) (Courtesy IBCC Digital Archive – Aircrew Remembered)

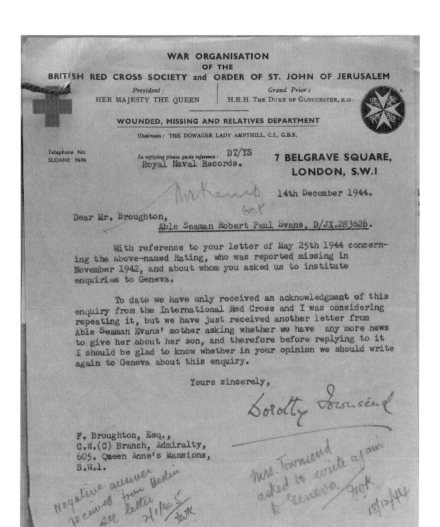

Red Cross letter dealing with the search for Evans' whereabouts (National Archives)

Memorial in Trandum Forest to those executed there.

R P Evans' headstone, Oslo Western Cemetery (Courtesy War Graves Photographic Project)

G M Sladen. England International Rugby cigarette card (Glyn L Evans collection)

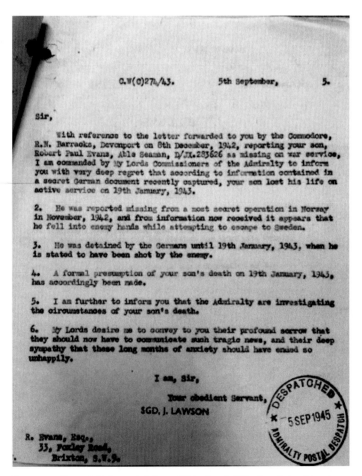

C.W(C)274/43.   5th September,   5.

Sir,

With reference to the letter forwarded to you by the Commodore, R.N. Barracks, Devonport on 8th December, 1942, reporting your son, Robert Paul Evans, Able Seaman, D/JX.283626 as missing on war service, I am commanded by My Lords Commissioners of the Admiralty to inform you with very deep regret that according to information contained in a secret German document recently captured, your son lost his life on active service on 19th January, 1943.

2.   He was reported missing from a most secret operation in Norway in November, 1942, and from information now received it appears that he fell into enemy hands while attempting to escape to Sweden.

3.   He was detained by the Germans until 19th January, 1943, when he is stated to have been shot by the enemy.

4.   A formal presumption of your son's death on 19th January, 1943, has accordingly been made.

5.   I am further to inform you that the Admiralty are investigating the circumstances of your son's death.

6.   My Lords desire me to convey to you their profound sorrow that they should now have to communicate such tragic news, and their deep sympathy that these long months of anxiety should have ended so unhappily.

I am, Sir,

Your obedient Servant,
SGD. J. LAWSON

R. Evans, Esq.,
33, Foxley Road,
Brixton, S.W.9.

Letter to Evans' father advising of his death (National Archives)

The War Medals of Leif Andreas Larsen

Norwegian

1. War Cross with Sword and Star 2. St Olav's Medal with Oak Branch
3. War Medal with Three Stars 4.Participation Medal 1939 - 1945
5. King Håkon VII 70 Year Medal

British

6. Distinguished Service Order 7. Distinguished Service Cross
8. Conspicuous Gallantry Medal 9. Distinguished Service Medal and Bar

Other Awards

10. Medal of Freedom (USA) 11. Finnish War Medal

The only known photo of Robert Paul Evans, from the book 'Chariots of the Sea', by Pamela Mitchell. In this, the caption gives Evans the rank of Leading Seaman which, given his short time in the service, cannot be correct. The indications are that Evans was rated Ordinary Seaman, made up to Able Bodied specifically for his role in Operation Title.

A 1930 photograph of Chiltern Court, the extensive block of apartments etc. above Baker Street Station, built in 1929 to the design of of the architect, Charles Walter Clark FRIBA, for the Metropolitan Railway Company.

tramps and wasters who wandered around eating decent folk's food. She became very agitated and her eyes shone with rage as she showered them with curses and abuse. The Englishmen stared in amazement at this fantastic creature. Larsen tried to reply but he might have spared himself the trouble. The woman got more and more excited and in the end stood shaking her fists at them. They had to give up.'

There is little doubt this was the woman at Brendmo [see Notes 4], of whom we shall later learn more. In the meantime, following Larsen's official report the SOE and Admiralty began their efforts to find out if Able Seaman Evans was dead or alive, and to discover his whereabouts or his fate. The search was to go on for over two years, his parents waiting anxiously at home in Brixton for news of their younger son.

Before moving on, this will perhaps be a suitable place to relate a tale that came to the author from Jorunn Melhus, whom we met in the fourth paragraph of this chapter. As a local folk singer from Frosta, Jorunn came into contact some twenty years ago with another singer, Annie Synnøve Skogseth, who was born in 1927. Annie's father, Arne Haugen (1898–1960), was a sailor and an active member of the Norwegian resistance movement during the German occupation. He was employed between 1933 and 1955 by Frosta Dampskibsselskab, a small shipping company running a service of vessels trading in Trondheimsfjord, connecting remote islands with mainland settlements. Haugen had a house at Faanes (Fånes) on the fjord's coast, a few miles north of Breivika. Annie was old enough in 1942 to have some understanding of what was going on when, she recalled, Leif

Larsen and his men stayed for one night at the house, or perhaps merely made a brief stop there. There is no written record of the event and Annie passed away some while ago, so its veracity cannot be guaranteed, although it is well within the bounds of possibility. The presence among the big farms on Frosta of Norwegian members of the Nasjonal Samling (NS), the movement sympathetic to the Nazi cause, made Haugen's actions in aiding Larsen and his party a dangerous enterprise. He was eventually betrayed in October 1944 by a member of the Rinnanbanden, a notorious group of Norwegian Gestapo agents. In their hands, Haugen was tortured and placed in solitary confinement in the Gestapo prison at Falstad run by Gerhard Flesch under Heimlich Fehlis. It would not be until the German occupation came to an end, on 8 May 1945, that Arne Haugen was freed. Flesch and Fehlis were later 'Called to Account', as I relate later in the chapter of that name.

Chapter 11

Evans – Dead or Alive?

As we have read in Larsen's report, he crossed the border from Norway into Sweden on Friday, 6 November 1942. Ten days later, on the 16th, he was in Stockholm giving a verbal account of the events surrounding his escape to Mr Nielsen of the British Legation there. The following message would have been based on that account:

'MOST SECRET
'OPERATION TITLE

'*From* – ADMIRAL (SUBMARINES)

'Northways, London, N.W.3

'*Date* – 20th November, 1942. *No.*2667/SN.04349

'*To* – SECRETARY OF THE ADMIRALTY

'With reference to paragraph 2(c) of Naval Attache, Stockholm's message timed 1212/16/11, it is requested that the next of kin of A.B. R.P. EVANS, Official No. D/FX88794 (R.G. EVANS of 125 VASSAL ROAD, BRIXTON, LONDON, S.W.9 – relationship – Father) may be informed that Evans is missing.

'2. It is not yet known if he was wounded or killed.

'3. At the time, he was engaged on Most Secret Operation 'TITLE'.

Ashbourne

'REAR-ADMIRAL

In the confusion that surrounded the shooting incident on the night of 5 November, it was very much a case of every man for himself. As we have seen, Larsen's later, written report of 28 November stated: 'I was too far in front to see what happened to AB Evans. I asked Sergeant Craig about Evans, and he said that Evans was lying in the road, either wounded or killed by the policeman.' Tebb's report, meanwhile, stated: 'I thought Evans must be dead, so I ran off.' From these reports, it would appear that no one in Larsen's party actually checked to see if Evans was dead or alive. In the absence of proof positive, Evans' parents were to be advised, as authorized by Rear Admiral Ashbourne, that their son was 'missing'. At the bottom of the above memorandum is a handwritten note, dated 5/12 and initialled by F. Broughton, which reads: 'Devonport instructed to report Evans missing on war service.' A letter to that effect was sent by the Commodore, RN Barracks, Devonport, to Mr and Mrs Evans on 8 December 1942.

A contradiction of the two statements above, by Larsen and Tebb, appears in Saelen's book *None But The Brave*, where he writes: 'The men examined him [Evans] and Larsen realized he would have to be left behind. There were hurried handshakes with the injured man and then they fled.' Although published in 1947, five years after the event, the book is considered to have been based on Larsen's verbal account, as dictated to and recorded by Saelen. This version could not differ more from Larsen's contemporary written report.

On file, and dated two days after Rear Admiral Ashbourne's memorandum, with apparently conclusive information regarding AB Evans, is the letter below from Chiltern Court, HQ of the

Scandinavian Branch of SOE to Northways, HQ Admiral (Submarines):

        'MOST SECRET AND PERSONAL.

'To	From
'Captain Lord Ashbourne, R.N.,	154 Chiltern Court
	[see Notes]
'Northways,	Baker Street, N.W 1
'Swiss Cottage	
	22nd November 1942
'JSW/2132	

'Dear …

'A telegram has been received from our branch in Stockholm which reports the receipt of confirmation that A.B. EVANS was dead when he was found.

'The telegram goes on to say:-

'"It is known by Germans that his party entered Trondheimfjord in fishing vessel which was sunk in only 3 fathoms and then salved. Vessel was found to contain large quantity of arms, ammunition and food, also asbestos suits with masks, all covered by peat sacks."

'Yours …'

The veracity of this report regarding Evans was obviously either doubted or considered by Admiral (Submarines) to be unsubstantiated, and thus no authority was given for a revision of circumstances to be passed to Mr and Mrs Evans regarding their son. File No. ADM358/2199, to be found at the National

Archives, Kew, reveals the extensive efforts made to trace the whereabouts and fate of Evans. A file note dated 22 April 1944, written and signed by G.C. Phillips pp Admiral (Submarines), ends by saying: 'No objection is seen to instituting enquiries through the British Red Cross Society to ascertain Ordinary [*sic*] Seaman Evans' fate.'

Accordingly, F. Broughton of CW (Casualties) Branch, Admiralty, based at Queen Anne's Mansions, St James' Park, London, wrote to Mrs Dorothy Townsend of the British Red Cross Society, 7 Belgrave Square, SW1, on 25 May 1944:

'I should be much obliged if enquiries could be instituted concerning Robert P Evans, Able Seaman, D/JX. 283626. This rating was one of a small party which landed in Norway on 1st November 1942 and is officially regarded as missing. Two reports concerning him have been received. Firstly that he was wounded and taken prisoner, but died subsequently in the mountains, and secondly that he had been taken to Levanger Hospital and later moved to the Red Cross Hospital at Trondheim.'

Dorothy Townsend replied on 30 May: 'In reply to your letter of May 25th asking if we would make enquiries through Geneva regarding the above-named rating, who has been missing in Norway since November 1942, I now enclose a copy of the letter we have sent to the International Red Cross, for your information.' That letter, addressed to Madame A. Morier, Comite International de la Croix Rouge, Geneva, read:

'Can enquiries be made through Berlin for Robert P. EVANS, Able Seaman D/JX.283626 who has been missing since November 1942 and believed to be in German hands: it appears he was wounded and might have possibly been taken to a hospital in the neighbourhood of Trondheim. We should be glad to have any definite information you may be able to obtain from Germany.'

Over six month later, on 14 December 1944, Dorothy Townsend wrote again to F. Boughton at the Admiralty:

'With reference to your letter of May 25th 1944 concerning the above-named Rating, who was reported missing in November 1942, and about whom you asked us to institute enquiries to Geneva. To date we have only received an acknowledgement of this enquiry from the International Red Cross and I was considering repeating it, but we have just received another letter from Able Seaman Evans' mother asking whether we have any more news to give her about her son, and therefore before replying to it I should be glad to know whether in your opinion we should write again to Geneva about this enquiry.'

From the above correspondence we can see that, not for the first time, Mrs Evans had resorted to writing to the Red Cross, her most recent letter probably having been sent in the first week of December 1944. By now, two long years had elapsed since she and her husband had first been advised by the Commodore,

Devonport, that their son was 'missing'. Two pencilled notes appear at the bottom of the Red Cross letter. One, written in hope and dated 18 December, reads: 'Mrs Townsend asked to write again to Geneva'; the other, later, one of despair, reads: 'Negative letter received from Berlin see letter dated 2nd January 1945.' The letter referred to was further correspondence from Dorothy Townsend advising CW (C) that a letter had been received from the International Red Cross dated 24 November 1944. It read: 'Reference your letter 31.5.44. (Royal Navy Records) the German authorities have replied negatively concerning the fate of Able Seaman Robert P. EVANS D/JX.283626.'

The response of F. Broughton at CW (C) to this latest news was a redoubling of effort, beginning with a file note two weeks later:

'It is felt that the matter should be further pursued as, in view of the special nature of the operation, it is possible that the German Authorities would consider him to have forfeited his rights as a member of the armed forces and regard him as a civilian offender or saboteur, and a routine enquiry from the Red Cross would not produce the desired result. Captain Mitchell of P.W. 2 Section at the War Office has been contacted and agreed that this is possible and that a more definite reply may be forthcoming if a request for information is made to the German High Command through the Protective Power.'

No objection was seen to this proposal, so on 7 February 1945, D.J. Ackner of the Naval Law Branch wrote to A.G. Ponsonby Esq. of the Prisoners of War Department at the Foreign Office. Having outlined the facts of Operation Title, the conflicting reports regarding the whereabouts and fate of AB Evans and the negative responses from the German authorities, the letter went on: 'I should be greatly obliged if you would take the necessary action.'

Taking into account the chaotic state of affairs under which the whole of Western Europe was at that time, it was remarkable that any response should be received. It would have come as little surprise that the matter, while being dealt with in a diplomatic manner, met only with a note from the Swiss legation in Germany dated 28 March 1945 to the effect that 'the German Foreign Office has been requested to make the desired investigations'.

With this avenue of enquiry having been explored, F. Broughton of CW (C) admitted four months later in his file note of 10 July 1945: 'In view of the cessation of hostilities in Europe it is felt that the enquiries concerning the fate of Abe Seaman Evans which the Foreign Office requested the Protecting Powers to make will now be non-effective.' However, not being one to give up, Broughton, with one last cast of the dice, contacted both the Foreign Office in Norway and the naval officer in charge, Trondheim. No response from either appears on file. The trail for information on the fate of Able Seaman Robert Paul Evans had gone cold.

It was only after the end of the war in Europe that documents came to light with proof that Able Seaman Evans had in fact survived the shooting incident mentioned by Larsen and Tebb in their reports. The first document was a report, sworn by Frontier Policeman R.H. Knudsen. The report was sent by policeman I. Maraas to the Royal Norwegian Legation, and shows that Evans survived the shooting on 5 November 1942, to be captured the next day, 6 November:

'REPORT

'To The Royal Norwegian   From Policeman
Legation   I. Maraas 9/6 – 1943

'Nr 17 859 **Knudsen**, Ragnar Henry b. 10.2.1923 in
Drammen

'Frontier Policeman living in Langesgt. 6. Drammen

'Nothing of importance happened until November 5th
1942. About 7 pm there was a telephone call at the police
post from Brendmo farm saying that five highly suspicious
people had arrived at the farm asking for food and lodgings.
The woman on the farm, Mrs Brendmo, was alone at home
and was apparently very nervous of them. She said on the
telephone she had sent them on to Karlgaard, situated
300–400 metres higher up than Brendmo, nearer to
Sulstua where a post was. These men were thus sent from
Brendmo nearer to the post where the frontier police were
[emphasis in original].

'I and Petersen then went west to Karlgaard. I was wearing
civilian clothing while Petersen was in uniform. I brought
my service pistol, a Walter 7.65 pistol, and Petersen had
a gun. When we had walked about 300–400 metres we
met the five men on the road. Petersen was walking about
4–5 metres behind me. I said to Petersen that he should

keep back in order to prevent the five men from seeing that he wore uniform and had a gun. I presume that Petersen carried the gun in his hand, but I'm not quite sure how he carried it. I had my pistol in my right hand by my thigh. It was pitch dark in the evening. It was about 7.15 pm when we heard the five men. I am of the opinion the weather was fine. I spoke to the men and asked where they were going. At first they would not answer at all and I got suspicious. The men carried sticks in their hands, one each. They were ordinary sticks of the same length and thickness as a walking stick.

'I ordered them to drop their sticks and put their hands up. At first only two or three did so, the others followed reluctantly as if they did not quite understand what I said. I had pointed my pistol at them before I ordered them to put their hands up. The pistol was loaded and I released the safety catch as I pointed at them. When they did not answer, I ordered them to stand two and two behind each other. This order was obeyed. I said that they were to march to Sulstua [sic – Sulstan]. One of the men asked me where they were going and what was going to happen. I was however afraid that the men were dangerous and I was nervous that something was going to happen. I was afraid that the men were carrying arms and as there were five against two I felt certain that the men would put up a fight. The men exchanged a few remarks which I did not understand. I at once realized that some of them were English. Before they started to walk I told the men that

I and my friend were carrying arms and that we were going to use them if we found it necessary.

'The men made no answer. They started to walk towards Salstus [*sic*] walking two and two together behind each other. Petersen walked on the left-hand side of the first two men at about one metre distance and I walked behind the last one and had a good view of all the men. We walked like that for some time until it suddenly occurred to me that Petersen might be shot without my being able to prevent it, being too far to the rear. I went closer in to the left-hand side of the last man. I think that I was at a distance of only one metre from the man. I was thus walking just behind Petersen. I had my finger on the trigger. I don't know how Petersen held his gun. Suddenly a shot rang out from the front man on the left and I felt at once a pain on the right side of the stomach. I had been prepared for shooting and had walked sideways in order to make as small a target as possible – this trick I had learnt at the front. I fired my pistol immediately after the man had shot.

'I had only four bullets and fired them straight away. I aimed at the man who had fired the shot, but did not aim properly. I remember that I then tried to get across the road. When I reached the other side I collapsed and was left lying on a little hill. There was about ten metres of snow on the place and [it was] 6–7 degrees below. I was unconscious for a little while, I don't know how long, but I think it was only about five minutes. When I gained consciousness I discovered another man lying on the other side of the road approximately five metres away. I tried to get up but could not manage. When the other man saw that I was moving he said, 'Come here my friend.' He spoke with an accent and I understood he was not Norwegian.

'I asked in German if the man was wounded and he answered, 'Ja'. Nothing else was said. I heard the man groaning and trying to sit up. I was afraid that the other man would start to shoot and therefore tried to drag myself away. I came down to the valley and went by another route to Sulstan. I partly crawled and partly walked the whole way to Sulstan. I did not see any of the others. Petersen had also disappeared. It appeared later that Petersen had been so scared he had run away. He had gone to a Nazi-farmer by name ….. He had fired one shot which had hit the road. From Sulstan somebody telephoned for a doctor for me but as the doctor was not at home the lensman [local community leader, similar to a parish councillor in Britain], Sul, was fetched and he brought me by car to the hospital in Levanger.

'Petersen returned later in the evening to Sulstan, after I had been taken to the hospital and both the group chief and the Germans had been informed. The German guard of the Schutzpolizei were then at Sandvika close to the Swedish border and they were out patrolling the country near the frontier. The Germans found tracks in the snow from three men who had walked together across the frontier, and one single track that also led across the frontier. From this they assumed that four men had gone across to Sweden. The man who I had wounded had gone through the woods up the mountains to the north east and was found the following morning in a hut near the Drivsjø [modern-day Drevsjø]. Both German and Norwegian police were sent for. Two or three 'blue-police' arrived at the hut. They did not, however, attack it. Several other policemen were also sent up and overpowered the man. He turned out to be English. I think that Petersen told me that the Englishman had got one more wound in the other thigh before he was arrested. I had hit him in the one thigh when I fired at him. I do not know what happened to the Englishman. I only know that the Germans took charge of him.

'I received no reward for the incident.'

The above report came into the hands of Lieutenant Colonel J.S. Wilson (see Notes), Head of the Scandinavian Branch of the SOE. Wilson sent a copy to Lieutenant Colonel B. Øen (see Notes), Chief of Staff to CinC H. Riiser-Larsen, Norwegian Combined Army Air Force:

'MOST SECRET

'JSW/1426   31st July, 1943
'TO: LT.COL. B. ØEN   FROM: LT.COL. J.S. WILSON

'OPERATION 'TITLE'

'You may remember that in the withdrawal of the party from this MOST SECRET Operation, Quartermaster

Leif Larsen and his four companions were confronted by two Norwegian policemen almost on the frontier.

'I attach a copy of a report which 8627 has sent me. This report was rendered to the legation in Stockholm, and a copy may have already come to your notice.

'There is no doubt this affray was brought about by the woman at BRENDMO Farm telephoning information to the police.

'The policeman, Knudsen's part in the affair is hardly creditable in a loyal Norwegian, but it would appear that he has been handed over to the Swedish authorities after interrogation, and has, in point of fact, been interned by them.

'Apparently no further information has been received concerning the fate of EVANS, the wounded Naval Rating, after he was taken to LEVANGER.'

The woman at Brendmo farm is no doubt the bad-tempered old woman who, according to the author Saelen, showered Larsen's party with curses and abuse, and in the end stood shaking her fists at them.

The following note also makes it clear that Able Seaman Evans survived the shooting and was taken to hospital:

'S.O.E. Headquarters from Stockholm (8627)
4th December 1942
'TITLE

'As regards the fate of Evans, we first heard that his death was confirmed from a report that was furnished by 8633, as mentioned in my telegram 4443 of November 21st. Copy of this report is attached: we are unaware of its origin, and have refrained from pressing 8630 on this point. The concluding paragraph seems definitely to confirm that the boat was subsequently salvaged, though the reference to M.R.D. appears obscure.

'It was reported by Tebb that while dining at a restaurant here he was approached by a Norwegian who recognised him as an Englishman. In the course of subsequent conversation the Norwegian mentioned that five Englishmen had been making their way across Norway and four succeeded in getting through, while one was wounded and taken to hospital. As the Norwegian had expressed a desire to meet Tebb again, and had mentioned that he himself had come over from the Trondheim neighbourhood and was returning to Norway, we were at first uneasy as to his identity and took steps to establish this. It proved to be the man X of my telegram 4518 of December 2nd.

'This man had previously been in touch with us having had a somewhat chequered career, in that he made a number of trips to Norway, and was in danger of arrest by the Swedes because he had no residential permit, and was known to have been in and out of Norway.

'Some months ago he disappeared from our ken, but is now working actively for Y. We saw him after his meeting Tebb, and he told us the story embodied in our telegram 4506 of November 30th. His tale corresponds with the one we received from 8633 as far as the hut is concerned: apparently Evans must have made his way to the hut, which was the property of a loyal Norwegian who had a wireless and some arms concealed there. This man is said to have been arrested and sent to Germany.

'X is shortly to visit Norway again and will endeavour to find out further particulars about Evans. He was prepared to make an attempt to rescue him from hospital if it were at all possible and Evans could move, as he has good connections in the town where the hospital is situated and could hide Evans until he is able to undertake the journey over the frontier.

'I told him that naturally we would be delighted if such a thing were possible but that no attempt should be made which would involve reprisals. Our impression of X is that he has greatly improved and doubtless toughened by his recent experiences. He has no knowledge of what the TITLE party were engaged in, but was nevertheless enjoined to observe the greatest discretion about the whole matter.'

The concern expressed above by SOE regarding reprisals can well be imagined. From lessons learnt through similar situations elsewhere [see Notes 26 – Televåg, April 1942], it is likely that, had an attempt been made to rescue Evans from the hospital, the deaths of many innocent people at the hands of the Gestapo would have followed. Unfortunately for Evans, this was to be too great a sacrifice to be made for one person. Already, it would seem, from the fourth paragraph of the above report, one man was likely to pay a high price for having given (probably unknowingly) shelter to Evans.

From Frontier Policeman Knudsen's report of Evans' capture at the hut, it would seem that Evans was alone; no mention was made of a second person being there at the time police reinforcements appeared on the scene. The hut was no doubt searched, the incriminating items found, and the loyal Norwegian owner tracked down and arrested. But for Evans coming upon the hut, the owner's involvement – if such there was – in resistance activities would have continued undetected. The author has found no record of his name or his ultimate fate.

Between Karlgaard (Karlgarden), where Evans was shot, and the hut near Drivsjø, where he was found, is a distance of about 7km, or 4.35 miles. Described by Knudsen, this was 'through the woods and up the mountains to the north east'. Evans must have been rendered unconscious on receiving the gunshot wound as, after the event, Tebb was unsure whether Evans was dead or alive. After Knudsen had left the scene, Evans somehow managed to stagger that distance in the dark and must have felt fortunate to find shelter from the deep snow and in the temperature of '6–7 degrees below'. In shock and disorientated, separated from his companions, Evans had unfortunately headed north east, whereas the route to the Swedish border and safety lay directly to the east.

The police response to the discovery of Evans' whereabouts was somewhat out of proportion to the resistance he could have offered, with a knuckleduster as his only means of aggression or defence. That he received gunshot wounds to his other thigh tends to suggest that he was not prepared to surrender without a fight, although, to use a rugby analogy, the police may have got their retaliation in first. Larsen's report tells us that, upon leaving *Arthur*, 'All members of the party, both Norwegian and British, had a pistol.' A German propaganda document (see later) states that 'Evans had in his possession a revolver holster, as worn under the arm-pit'. This begs the question, what happened to Evans' pistol? We know that Larsen and Kalve had earlier given their pistols to the son of the farmer at Tretten. Larsen reports that later, after the shooting, Sergeant Craig gave his gun to Kalve. This provokes the, by now unanswerable, question as to why Evans and Craig did not take part in the shoot-out.

Through the work of the man, Agent X, it might have been expected that further news of Evans would be forthcoming, possibly of his recovery in hospital and perhaps of his subsequent treatment as a prisoner of war and transfer to a PoW camp in Germany. However, as we know, the trail to discover his whereabouts went cold, despite the best efforts of the authorities, who worked so hard to keep next of kin informed in these circumstances.

At this juncture, the last positive news of Able Seaman Evans was the note dated 4 December 1942 from SOE headquarters, with the report from Agent X of him being in hospital. Even after the capitulation of German forces in Norway on 8 May 1945, the fate of AB Evans was still unclear, as shown in this sworn statement which came to light at that time, from Egil Lindheim, chief of the Norwegian Police, Trondheim:

'(a) I am a lawyer by profession, [and] during the German occupation of Norway from 1st July 1942 until the capitulation I was chief of the uniformed police at TRONDHEIM. My rank was Oberstleutnant. I was responsible to the Police President at TRONDHEIM. I was a member of the N.S. and since the capitulation I have been in the custody of the Norwegian Police.

'(b) In the autumn of 1942, I cannot remember the exact date, but believe it was the end of October, a report was received and passed to me stating that a policeman had been shot near SUUL in VERDAL.

'(c) An officer and four men from the criminal police were sent to SUUL, later I with two cars and 10 or 12 men, uniformed police, also proceeded to SUUL, and a leutnant and 30 men of the uniformed police were ordered to follow as soon as possible.

'(d) Investigation revealed by means of tracks that five men had been present at the shooting and that four had gone eastwards and one man on his own. The tracks were followed up and of the party of four three had crossed the border and one had gone off into the woods.

'(e) The next day enquiries were made among the peasants and all the farms and huts in the locality were searched in the attempt to find this man.

'(f) On the day following a man was found in a mountain hut. As he opened the door the police thinking he would shoot fired at him and wounded him in the thigh.

'(g) The man was then brought in a wagon to SULL to me by the Norwegian Police and the district doctor attended to his wound.

'(h) His pockets had been emptied and the following handed to me:
   a) One knuckleduster
   b) Some Swedish and Norwegian money
   c) A silk handkerchief on which was printed a map of
      N & S Trøndelag
   d) A notebook with his name and English address
   e) An English Half Crown coin

'(i) He had no identity card or disc in his possession and the paper with his name and address as far as I can remember, contained no number or rank. I cannot remember his name.

'(j) He was dressed in [garments] which as far as I can describe were a jacket and trousers, blue in colour and lined with the kind of material used in sleeping bags. I am fairly sure that this dress was in two parts, jacket and trousers, the colour may have been grey but I think it was blue. There were no badges of any description.

'(k) I talked with the man a little and he told me he had come to NORWAY in a fast motorboat, which had been wrecked, and he was attempting to get to SWEDEN.

Later I learnt that he had come in an attempt to sink the 'Tirpitz'.

'(l)   The Englishman was then taken to TRONDHEIM by two of the Sicherheitspolizei* and I saw no more of him.'

[*SiPo, the state political and criminal investigation security agency, merged in 1939 into the RSMO, Reich Security Main Office.]

As we shall see, it was not until 28 August 1945 that a further report regarding the fate of AB Evans came to the attention of F. Broughton at CW (C) at the Admiralty. After Operation Title, SOE continued to organize sabotage activities in Norway. One mission in particular, code named Operation Freshman, is described in the next chapter, although the relevance of this mission to the tale of AB Evans will seem obscure at this point.

Chapter 12

Operation Freshman

The Allied mission to destroy the Vemork heavy water plant, Operation Freshman, began on 19 November 1942, a little over three weeks after *Arthur* had sailed off on Operation Title. While in no way connected to Operation Title, it shared the similarities of having a target in Norway and ultimately failing to achieve its objective through circumstances beyond the control of the men involved. Five members of Operation Freshman and one from Operation Title were to meet later. Two days after the launch of Operation Freshman, a message was broadcast by German wireless: 'On the night of 19/20th November two British bombers, each towing one glider, flew into Southern Norway. One bomber and both gliders were forced to land. The sabotage troops they were carrying were *put to battle and* wiped out to the last man.' This summary would be correct in almost every detail if one were to omit the four words which the author has set here in italics.

From information received through the efforts of the SIS and members of the Norwegian resistance, the Allies had become aware of a hydro-electric facility in Norway manufacturing fertilizer with, as a by-product, deuterium oxide – or 'heavy water'. This was being shipped to Germany and there put to use by German scientists in their attempts to produce a new source of power through atomic fission. Later, it became apparent to these scientists that the power could be utilized to produce an atomic bomb, which would give the Nazi war machine an unassailable advantage over the Allies. Something had to be done to prevent this happening.

The location of the hydro-electric station was the Vemork Norske Hydro plant at Rjukan, a remote spot in a landscape that was hostile to the point of being almost inaccessible and, given its importance, heavily guarded. The station harnessed the power to be generated from the water flowing with such natural force from the Hardangervidda down into the Vestfjord, with its steep cliffs and deep gorges. A reconnaissance mission in October 1942, code named Grouse, consisted of four Norwegian SOE commandos who were dropped by parachute on to the Hardanger Plateau. It was from the information they provided, collected under the most arduous of conditions, that SOE decided it would be possible to mount an operation (Freshman) to put the plant out of commission.

The ambitious scheme, using methods untried and untested under combat conditions, was to land a party of thirty Royal Engineers at the location identified by the Grouse reconnaissance party, as close to the plant as practicable, from where they would make their way on foot to the target, destroy it with explosives and make good their escape to neutral Sweden. From the outset, this had all the hallmarks of a one-way ticket, but nevertheless, volunteers came forward and preparations began in earnest. Two Horsa gliders, each with two pilots and fifteen sappers, were to be towed by two Halifax bombers of 38 Group RAF, each with a crew of seven, the mission thus consisting of a total of forty-eight men.

Halifax A – Apple was piloted by Squadron Leader A.B. Wilkinson and accompanied by Group Captain T.B. Cooper, while Halifax B – Baker was piloted by Flight Lieutenant A.R. Parkinson, RCAF, with Pilot Officer G.W. Sewell de Gency, RAFVR.

In one glider, in overall command of the mission, was Lieutenant David Alexander Methven, commissioned into the Royal Engineers in October 1941, who had volunteered for the operation. He had been awarded the George Medal for bravery in July 1942, before transferring to 9th Field Company (Airborne) Royal Engineers. He was 20 years old. Second in command, in the other glider, was Lieutenant A.C. Allen. Piloting one Horsa were Sergeants Strathdee and Doig of the Glider Pilot Regiment, the other being flown by Pilot Officer Davis and Sergeant Fraser of the Royal Australian Air Force. On board were men from 9th Field Company (Airborne) RE and 261 Field Park Company (Airborne) RE.

RAF Skitten in Caithness, north east Scotland a base for RAF Coastal Command was the setting-off point. At around 6.00 pm, in weather conditions far from ideal and which in normal circumstances would have seen the departure delayed, the two Halifax bombers took off, each with their Horsa glider in tow.

From the outset, all that could go wrong did go wrong, beginning with the loss of the communication facility between the bomber pilots and those in the gliders, making a difficult task even more arduous during what was estimated to be a three-hour trip. As the flight continued, the weather conditions worsened beyond those forecast, and deteriorating visibility made it impossible for the prearranged glider landing site to be identified. This was despite the provision of a short-range transponder system, a ground-operated signal transmitter with corresponding receiver equipment in the bombers, which should have made certain of arrival over the correct spot. As the bombers continued to circle in their attempt to find the landing spot for the gliders, the problem was taken from them when, due to the severe icing at the height and in the conditions prevailing, the tow ropes snapped. In this most inhospitable region, with virtually zero visibility owing to a thick ground fog, the glider pilots' chances of a successful landing – never an easy task in the best of circumstances – disappeared. The gliders crashed some miles apart, killing both pilots in each and some of the sappers, leaving others badly injured and with just a few dazed survivors. Halifax A – Apple managed to make it back to base in Scotland, but Halifax B – Baker crashed into a Norwegian mountainside, instantly killing all seven on board.

From one crashed glider, two men made their way to a nearby farm to enlist help for the injured. Despite the language barrier, the locals quickly understood what was required and made their way up the rocky hillside to the crash site. It was inevitable that this activity in an otherwise quiet location should stir up a force of German occupation troops, who, upon arriving at the crash site, immediately ordered the Norwegians to return to their homes. The dead, the injured and the other survivors were taken down the hillside and then to the German garrison at Slettbo. From here they were later taken one-by-one to a nearby quarry, where they were shot as a result of Hitler's Commando Order of the previous month. The bodies were buried in a shallow grave, an action witnessed by a local Norwegian who, fearing reprisals, said nothing to the authorities until the German capitulation some two-and-a-half years later. Following exhumation and identification, the bodies were given a proper burial.

The second glider crash produced more fatalities, leaving just four badly injured and five other survivors. German troops were again quickly on the scene, taking the four injured sappers to hospital. Here they were brutally treated and murdered, their bodies being dumped at sea and never recovered. The five survivors, now prisoners of the Germans, were taken to Grini Prison in Oslo (see Notes). They were Lance Corporal Jackson (age 21) and Sappers Bonner (25), Walsh (21), Blackburn (28) and White (23). Taking into account the seven aircrew safely back at RAF Skitten, the death toll from Operation Freshman at that point stood at thirty-six out of forty-eight.

Chapter 13

Grini Prison and Trandum Forest

Shortly before the German invasion of Norway, the Norwegian authorities had completed the construction of a women's prison at Grini, just outside Oslo. The modern structure, designed for 700 prisoners, was first used by the Germans to house Norwegian officers captured during the initial fighting in 1940. On 14 June 1941, a convoy of trucks unloaded there 150 men who had been arrested for various anti-German activities. They were the first of almost 20,000 men and women who, at one time or another, would experience imprisonment under Nazi German conditions at Grini.

Grini was designated by the occupying force as a 'police detention camp' rather than a 'concentration camp'. The rules and treatment were harsh, but they never approached the barbaric inhumanity of the concentration camps in Germany, Poland and Czechoslovakia. Compared with these, Grini offered an almost benign but nevertheless to be feared existence. Here, prisoners were given responsibility for their own administration, albeit under strict German control: which meant Gestapo leaders and SS guards. Norwegians always formed the majority of prisoners, but citizens from other occupied countries and from Britain, Russia and America were sometimes incarcerated there too.

As the Norwegian resistance movement grew, and the number of arrests increased, the capacity at Grini had to be expanded.

Prison labour was employed to clear away the surrounding trees and to build huts, each with nine rooms housing fourteen prisoners. An electric fence surrounded the entire area, so that Grini now looked even more like a German concentration camp, although accommodation was marginally better. The main building became partly the women's prison (some 600 women spent time at Grini) and partly a confinement section, Cell 415, for prisoners who, in the eyes of the Gestapo, had committed the most serious crimes. The isolation cell, known as '*Dødens veteværelse*' (Death's waiting room), was for prisoners who were condemned – or were about to be condemned – to death. Death was a frequent visitor to Grini – both directly and by way of transportation to concentration camps in Germany.

It was to Grini Prison that the five surviving Royal Engineers from Operation Freshman were delivered on 21 November 1942: Lance Corporal Jackson and Sappers Bonner, Walsh, Blackburn and White. They were housed in one of the wooden huts behind the main building, and for the first three weeks were the only British prisoners held there. Then, on 14 December, they were joined by another British prisoner, recently discharged from hospital having sufficiently recovered from his gunshot wounds: none other than Able Seaman Robert Paul Evans, captured on 7 November. In an earlier chapter, we learnt from the statement sworn by Egil Lindheim, Chief of the Norwegian Police, that, after capture, Evans had been handed over to SiPo, the state political and criminal investigation security agency. In the hands of various divisions of German intelligence, Evans would have been interrogated repeatedly, both while in hospital and subsequently. By this time, however, Evans would have little to tell his interrogators that they had not already found out for themselves. The Norwegian fishing boat, *Arthur*, had not sunk as planned, but had drifted in a waterlogged state into shallow water north of the island of Tautra, to be discovered there by a German shore-line patrol. The cables attached to its keel and the false compartment with its tell-tale contents had given up their secrets.

We now jump forward two years to the point where, immediately upon securing victory in Europe (VE Day) on 8 May 1945, the Allies set about the enormous task of bringing to account those German individuals known or thought to have been involved in the perpetration of war crimes and crimes against humanity. Documents were quickly seized across Germany and throughout those territories that had been under Nazi occupation, to prevent their destruction and to be used in evidence. In addition to these documents, thousands of statements were taken from members of all branches of the German armed forces, and also from those who had suffered at their hands. Copies of these documents and statements slowly made their way back through Allied intelligence agencies to the units which would find them of most interest and use in their on-going enquiries. By this means, several such statements came into the hands of SOE, SIS and the Admiralty in relation to Operation Title, and in particular relating to the fate of Able Seaman R.P. Evans.

Marked 'SECRET' and headed 'WAR CRIMES', a letter dated 13 August 1945 was received by F. Broughton, CW (Casualties), at the Admiralty. It had come from Spring Gardens, Cockspur Street, SW1, and was signed by a colonel for the Military Deputy, JAG (Judge Advocate General of the Forces). It read: 'I enclose herewith a captured enemy document which I have received from P.W.2 [the War Office] relating to proposed German reprisals for the Kharkov War Crimes Trials [see Notes 1]. Paragraphs 2, 3, 4, and 5 may be of interest to you.' The six-page document, signed 'REICHEL', was dated 12 January 1944 and marked 'MOST SECRET DOCUMENT – To be submitted to Chief, High Military Command via Chief Foreign Dept/Security. Re. Counter-Action to Kharkov Fake Trial. For exploitation for propaganda purposes following cases come into consideration.'

Paragraph 2 was certainly of interest to Broughton, and while it gave him the news of Evans, he had sought for two years, sadly it was not the outcome for which he had hoped. Headed 'Acts of violence committed by Seaman EVANS on his flight after the planned attack on the battleship TIRPITZ', the item detailed the failed 'British Commando' raid, the hard fight with the Norwegian frontier officials and, it continued,

'the discovery of EVANS on 7.11 in a locked hut when, owing to resistance offered, he received two slight bullet wounds to his upper thigh. Evans had in his possession a revolver holster, as worn under the arm-pit, also a knuckle-duster. **He was shot on 19.1.1943 in accordance with the Führer's order.'**

The full facts of the case gradually came to light. Early on the morning of 19 January 1943, five days after his twenty-first birthday, Able Seaman Evans, together with the five Royal

Engineers, were roused from their prison cells and informed they were to be taken immediately before a higher German authority for yet more questioning. This, they were told, would involve a journey through a sensitive military area, so their eyes were to be bandaged and their hands tied behind their back. In the freezing cold of a Norwegian winter's morning, they were loaded into two lorries under armed guard and driven to Trandum Forest, a journey which would have taken around two hours. What happened after Evans and the five sappers arrived at Trandum Forest is recorded in several statements which are to be found in the subsequently declassified 'Most Secret' files held at the National Archives, Kew. Below are two statements from Oscar Hans, and another from Wilhelm Esser, which reveal the grim facts and the parts they played in them:

'Statement of Witness

'I, OSCAR HANS, having been duly sworn, wish to make the following statement.

'My full name is OSCAR HANS, I was born in WOLLMERINGEN, KREISHOFEN on the 6th January 1910. Before the war I worked at the S.D. [Sicherheitsdienst, the Security Service] in Germany, at the time of the capitulation I worked at the Gestapo Headquarters in Oslo. I had the rank of HAUPTSTURMFUHRER in the S.S. I was a member of the N.S.D.A.P. [Nazi Party] In winter 1942–1943 I got a written order from FEHLIS that the mentioned English citizens had been sentenced to death for sabotage, I think there were six of them mentioned. I got this written order in FEHLIS'S office. REINHART was also present. FEHLIS ordered me to bring the prisoners from GRINI to the execution place at TRANDUM. I was to tell the prisoners that they should be led to a German delegation and therefore must have their eyes bandaged. They were to be shot on the order: 'ACHTUNG'. I received this order in the evening, I went to GRINI with an execution squad the same evening and the prisoners were shot early in the morning. I also got the order that these were very important persons and that I was responsible for them with the cost of my head. I carried the orders out. I gave the order to shoot and afterwards ordered the execution squad to bury the bodies in a grave that had been dug the day before. The prisoners never knew they were going to be shot, because the execution squad was fully prepared when the prisoners arrived at the grave. BEHNECKE acted as interpreter. He followed the lorries to TRANDUM. I reported the completion of the execution to FEHLIS when I returned. I was instructed by FEHLIS to conduct the matter with the utmost secrecy.

'I have given this statement quite voluntarily, it has been read to me and it is true.

'[Signed] OSCAR HANS
'Sworn before me at AKERSHUS jail [see Notes 1] on the 11th day of August, 1945.

'[Signed] A.P. CARDWELL, Capt., for Major (There being no Fd. Offr. present)

'Witnessed and interpreted   [Signed] A BANG
ANDERSEN'

'Further witness statement by Oscar Hans,
'made on 18th October 1945,

'Akershus Prison, [see Notes] Oslo before A P Cardwell, Capt., R.A.

'When the grave had been prepared in accordance with regulations, I ordered the execution squad to march off to the execution area. When the prisoners arrived on the troop training place they were blindfolded with white bandages which they retained during the execution. When the execution squad had taken up their position at about 5–8 metres distance from the edge of the grave, the prisoners were taken to the grave and placed so that they stood face to face with the execution squad. Three rifles were directed at each of the condemned. When the rifles were brought to the 'Ready' by a signal, the order to fire followed on the command 'Achtung', and this was carried out in one salvo. As the result of the salvo was instantaneous death of all the condemned, the execution squad marched off to the vehicles and another squad took over the filling in and smoothing of the grave.

'The whole squad, after the grave had been smoothed down, started off for Oslo still in the forenoon. I myself had immediately to make a report concerning the completion of the execution to Commandant Fehlis in view of a further report to the Reichskommissar, the higher SS and Polizeiführer Rediess, as also to the Reichssicherheitshauptamt.

'The members of the squad on their arrival in Oslo were pledged again to special strict secrecy. As I have already said in my first interrogation, I did not know at this period that the condemned were British nationals and soldiers.

'I have made this statement voluntarily. I have read it through and it is true.

'[Signed] HANS

'Sworn statement of Wilhelm Esser

'I, WILHELM KARL JOHANN JOSEF ESSER, having been duly sworn, wish to make the following statement;

'a)   I was born in Norway on 15th January 1908 and before the war I lived in Kiel. On the 30th April 1940, I came to Norway and from that time until the Capitulation I was attached to the CO of the Security Police and SD in Oslo.

'b)   In Nov. or Dec. in the year 1942 I went to the Prison Grini in company with the interpreter X to interrogate 5 Englishmen. I interrogated these men 3 or 4 hours each day during 5 days. They told me that they had been the passengers of a glider which had crashed – as they learnt later on – near Helleland. They wore blue pullovers and blue trousers. I did not see the men again until the day I heard fragments of a conversation between them and the interpreter X as I walked up and down the corridor at Grini.

'c)   At about the same time I interrogated the 5 Englishmen at Grini I also interrogated another Englishman at Victoria Terasse [see Notes 1] in Oslo. He told me by the interpreter that his name was Evens [*sic*]. I saw Evens 4 times but did not interrogate him each time.

'd)   One night in January 1943 I drove with Hans and X to Grini and there I heard X speaking separately with the two groups of Englishmen. At this time the Englishmen had their eyes bandaged. Their hands were tied behind their backs. The Englishmen were then led out and brought into two lorries. Hans and I then entered a motor car that was driven by Ettling. This car led on, followed by two lorries, and the last one was another motor car. From Grini we led this column of cars to Trandum.

'e)   The night was very cold. There was snow and ice and the whole drive lasted two hours. As we arrived at Trandum we halted near the Lagerunterkunft [stores building] and there we should either wait for an order or the arrival of the cars should be reported to the Camp Administration. After a short while the column proceeded and halted near a side road running from the main road. It was still dark, and during the halt brandy and cigarettes were issued, and the Englishmen received some as well. At dawn we descended from the cars, whereas the lorries proceeded along the side road and halted near the artillery position. The men who had come by motor car walked on foot up to the lorries. This group was composed of the occupants of the second motor car, and me, Hans and – I think – Ettling. We waited about a quarter of an hour until daylight.

'f) The execution squad stepped out of the cars and went over to the place of execution in the wood. This execution squad was led by Hans. About 15 minutes after the execution squad had left the lorries, the prisoners were taken separately from the lorries, and each led by two men from the Sonderkommando [Special Squad] over to the edge of the previously dug grave. I cannot remember the names of those who led the Englishmen to the graves. Behnecke and some others, probably drivers, stayed on by the lorries and I went slowly towards the execution squad where I positioned myself 10 M [metres] behind the second row of men. I believe I went together with Hans. I saw that the execution squad was lined up in two rows. Two prisoners were already positioned in front of the grave and the rest were being led up. As soon as one prisoner had been positioned, the men who led him up moved off.

'g) When the last prisoner had been brought up to the grave and their guards had moved off, Hans went up to the left flank (as seen from my position) of the execution squad. He raised his right hand, and the rifles which had already been loaded were brought into aiming position. Then Hans gave the command 'FIRE', and the squad shot at the prisoners standing in front of the grave.

'h) The death sentence was not read to the prisoners because it had previously been decided that this should not be done and because they had been informed that they were to be placed before a military commission.

'i)   I am sure that the 5 Englishmen, shot at that time, were the ones I had interrogated in Grini and that their names were the following; Bonner, White, Walsh, Blackburn and Jackson. Of the five, four wore blue pullovers and blue trousers. The fifth man had his left arm in a sling, he wore a white shirt and blue trousers. This one was the biggest and his name was Blackburn. The sixth man was the one I had interrogated in Victoria Terrasse, whose name was Evans. He was dressed in grey coloured mackintosh with a belt, dark trousers, and was bare headed, wore collar and tie, but I do not remember the colour.

'j)   I had to go out there on order from Reinhardt, because I had interrogated the people on his order.

'k)   I am certain the following named took part in this action; I cannot with certainty say however if they took part in the execution, the guarding or the digging of the grave. [Eighteen names follow] The following were present, but

I am certain they did not take part in the execution. Thun, because he was standing guard on the left side, Runnfeld, because he was standing guard on the right side, Ettling, because, I believe, he stayed on by the car, and Valstab, because, as far as I remember, [he] was running around. As far as I remember now Runnfeld was in the car with us.

'l)   I have made this statement quite voluntarily. I have read it through and swear it is correct.

'[Signed] Wilhelm Esser

'Sworn by the above named
'Wilhelm Karl Johann Josef Esser
'Before me this 16th day of November
1945 at Akershus Prison [see Notes]
[Signed] John Humphries, Major
'Witnessed and interpreted:

'[Signed] L Lieven, Lt. I.C.'

The statements of both Esser and Hans were made over two years after the execution of Able Seaman Evans. What was happening between times on the home front?

Chapter 14

On the Home Front

Following the repatriation of the nine survivors of Operation Title from neutral Sweden to Britain, their individual reports were made without delay, from which the authorities concluded Able Seaman R.P. Evans should be officially posted 'Missing'. His parents, Ralph George and Rose Catherine Evans, were informed accordingly on 8 December 1942, with a promise that all steps possible would be taken to trace their son's whereabouts. Enquiries were made through all official channels available, chief of which was the International Red Cross Committee at Geneva. However, as Grini Prison was for the detainment of political prisoners, i.e. those classed by the German occupation force as undesirables or dissidents, rather than combatants, Evans could not be traced through the normal prisoner-of-war records system to which the International Red Cross had access.

It is likely that accompanying the letter to Mr and Mrs Evans would have been an official printed leaflet:

'ADVICE TO THE RELATIVE
OF A MAN WHO IS MISSING

'In view of the official notification that your relative is missing, you will naturally wish to hear what is being done to trace him.

'The Service Departments make every endeavour to discover the fate of missing men, and draw upon all likely sources of information about them.

'A man who is missing after an engagement may possibly be a prisoner of war. Continuous efforts are made to speed up the machinery whereby the names and camp addresses of prisoners of war can reach this country. The official means is by lists of names prepared by the enemy Government. These lists take some time to compile, especially if there is a long journey from the place of capture to a prisoners of war camp. Consequently "capture cards" filled in by the prisoners themselves soon after capture and sent home to their relatives are often the first news received in this country that a man is a prisoner of war. That is why we ask you in the accompanying letter to forward at once any card or letter you may receive, if it is the first news you have had.

'Even if no news is received that a missing man is a prisoner of war, endeavours to trace him do not cease. Enquiries are pursued not only among those who were serving with him, but also through diplomatic channels and the International Red Cross Committee at Geneva.

'The moment reliable news is obtained from one of these sources it is sent to the Service Department concerned. They will pass the news on to you at once if they are satisfied that it is reliable. It would be cruel to raise false hopes, such as may be raised if you listen to one or other possible channel of news, namely the enemy broadcasts. These are listened to by official listeners, working continuously night and day. The few names of prisoners given by enemy announcers are carefully checked. They are often misleading, and this is not surprising, for the object of the inclusion of prisoners' names in these broadcasts is not to help the relatives of prisoners, but to induce British listeners to hear some tale which otherwise they could not be made to hear. The only advantage of listening to these broadcasts is an advantage to the enemy.

'The official listeners can never miss any name included in an enemy broadcast. They pass every name on to the Service Department concerned. There, every name is checked, and in every case where a name can be verified, the news is sent direct to the relatives.

'There is, therefore, a complete official service designed to secure for you and to tell you all discoverable news about your relative. This official service is also a very human service, which well understands the anxiety of relatives and will spare no effort to relieve it.'

[reproduced with the kind permission of the University of Lincoln International Bomber Command Centre Digital Archive]

From the National Archives (File ADM 358/2199 Document 281/44), two brief notes indicate that in May 1944 enquiries were still being made:

'? Will F.O.S. please say what information if any has been received concerning him and whether he should still be regarded as "Missing".

'C W (Casualties) 13/5/44'

'Latest information received by Ad (Subs) from Norwegian sources dated 12/1/43 to the effect Evans was wounded and believed to have been taken to a Red Cross hospital in Trondheim. Consider in the circumstances he should continue to be listed as "Missing".

'Ad (Subs) 16.5.44'

As we know from the previous chapter, it was not until August 1945 that positive information regarding Evans was received, in a roundabout way, by CW (Casualties). This information was passed on to the Admiralty (Submarines) in the letter below:

'From C.W. (Casualties)

'The information contained on page 2, item 2, of the enclosed copy of a captured enemy document, the original received from the Judge Advocate General's Department having been passed to M Branch in the investigation of War Crimes, is the only definite evidence of this man's fate since he was reported missing in November, 1942.

'2. Previous to the receipt of this document, the only information available concerning Evans was furnished by F.O. (S) in his minute of 22nd April, 1944, but as the information (paragraph 5) was somewhat conflicting, the Rating was retained on the missing list pending the receipt of more definite information concerning him.

'3. In view of the circumstances of death now revealed, it is submitted to accept the information and to record Evans as having died on 19th January, 1943, and to inform his next of kin as in the enclosed letter.

[Signed]
'F Broughton
'CW (Casualties) 28th August, 1945'

The purpose of the captured enemy document referred to was to provide members of the German High Command with 'evidence', should the need arise, to enable them to justify the various executions that had taken place. By this time, ultimate defeat at the hands of the Allies was becoming more apparent and those who could see this were making preparations for the inevitable. Propaganda had played a large part in keeping the Nazi ideals at the forefront of the minds of the German armed forces while setbacks continued to mount. They had lost air superiority in the Battle of Britain, the U-boat menace had been nullified in the Battle of the Atlantic, their forces had been driven out of North Africa, they had lost support from the Italians, and the Russians had turned the tables on them. Individuals in high command were considering their personal position, and the propaganda here was intended to both ease their conscience and bolster their resolve.

As we have read, the document concluded: 'EVANS had in his possession a revolver holster, as worn under the arm-pit, also a knuckleduster. He was shot on 19.1.43 in accordance with the Führer's order.'

Being unarmed apart from a knuckleduster and having received three bullet wounds, it is difficult to imagine the exact nature of the 'acts of violence' committed by Able Seaman Evans referred to earlier in this document. Nevertheless, his fate had been sealed by Hitler's Commando Order issued just three months earlier following the raid on Sark, Operation Basalt.

CW (Casualties), as they had proposed on 28 August, wrote the following letter to Evans' father at 33 Foxley Road, Brixton, SW9:

'C.W. (C) 274/43.   5th September 1945

'Sir

'With reference to the letter forwarded to you by the Commodore, R.N. Barracks, Devonport on 8th December, 1942, reporting your son, Robert Paul Evans, Able Seaman, D/JX. 283626 as missing on war service, I am commanded by My Lords Commissioners of the Admiralty to inform you with very deep regret that according to information contained in a secret German document recently captured, your son lost his life on active service on 19th January, 1943.

'2. He was reported missing from a most secret operation in Norway in November, 1942, and from information now received it appears that he fell into enemy hands while attempting to escape to Sweden.

'3. He was detained by the Germans until 19th January, 1943, when he is stated to have been shot by the enemy.

'4. A formal presumption of your son's death on 19th January, 1943, has accordingly been made.

'5. I am further to inform you that the Admiralty are investigating the circumstances of your son's death.

'6. My Lords desire me to convey to you their profound sorrow that they should now have to communicate such tragic news, and their deep sympathy that these long months of anxiety should have ended so unhappily.

'I am, Sir,
'Your obedient Servant
'SGD J LAWSON'

CW (Casualties) closed their file on Able Seaman Evans on 4 September 1945 with a memorandum to all those departments that had been involved in the investigation into his fate, in particular to the British Red Cross Society and, importantly, to the Drafting Commander, RN Barracks, Devonport:

'Approval has been given to presume the death of Robert P. Evans, Able Seaman, D/JX283626, previously reported missing, to have occurred on 19th January 1943.'

The author has found no evidence to show that the exact circumstances of their son's death were ever communicated to Mr and Mrs Evans: it would have been hard enough for them to bear the news that he was dead after waiting in hope for almost two years. It is doubtful they could have been advised of their son's death earlier. Reports show that eleven mass graves were discovered in Trandumskogen (Trandum Forest) as early as May 1945, shortly after the German occupiers capitulated. In total, 173 Norwegians, six British and fifteen Soviet citizens were executed there and buried in unmarked graves. Many had been sentenced to death by the Germans, but a great number were subject to arbitrary execution.

Upon the graves being discovered, Norwegian citizens sentenced for treason, and leading members of the Norwegian national socialist party, NS, were forced to open the graves and exhume the bodies. The medical identification was led by a professor of forensic medicine, assisted by a dentist. The remains were cremated and interred; those of Evans and the five sappers must have been identified at that time for them to have received the engraved headstones that now stand in Oslo Western Civil Cemetery. In view of the number of bodies involved, it is perhaps to be expected that the identification and publication of the results thereof would have taken some considerable time, possibly beyond September 1945. With the identification of the sappers having been confirmed, the final death toll from Operation Freshman closed at forty-one out of forty-eight.

Also briefly held at Grini Prison in May 1943 were seven men of another Allied mission, Operation Checkmate. This was a raid using canoes, with limited success, on shipping at Haugesund,

Norway, by men of No. 14 (Arctic) Commando under Lieutenant John Godwin, RNVR. After capture and time at Grini, the seven were sent to Sachsenhausen concentration camp, where five were executed: yet more victims of Hitler's Commando Order. The remaining two were sent on to Belsen, where one was also executed while the other died of typhus. Operation Checkmate was another of those mentioned in the German secret document as evidence of Allied commando atrocities.

On 10 October 1954, a granite memorial was unveiled in Trandumskogen to those who lost their lives there, the ceremony being attended by Crown Prince Olav of Norway. The memorial, declared a Norwegian National Cultural Heritage Site on 5 May 2020, lists the names of the victims and bears a carved inscription in Norwegian, Russian and English that reads:

'IN THE COMBAT FOR FREEDOM
DURING THE 1940–1945 WAR
173 NORWEGIANS 15 SOVJET-
SUBJECTS AND 6 BRITONS WERE
HERE IN THE WOODS OF TRAN-
DUM EXECUTED BY THE ENEMY'

Chapter 15

Conclusions

A report on Operation Title was issued from the Norwegian Embassy in Sweden, dated 4 December 1942, barely a month after *Arthur*, its crew and passengers first arrived in Norwegian waters. The final part of the report, headed 'Conclusions', states:

'It would seem that the Germans had not yet grasped that any Norwegians were involved, as it was thought the party engaged in the shooting incident were entirely British; but the fact that the boat did not sink after being scuttled, but was salved and found to contain inter alia diving suits, coupled with the fact that the pass issued to the boat at the controls was never left with the shore authorities as would have been the case with a genuine vessel, should enable the German Intelligence service to piece the plan together.

'The Swedish authorities have apparently been willing to accept the escape story at its face value, and no difficulty has been raised to the despatch of our men to the UK as escaped prisoners of war.

'Conclusions

'1. As regards the preparatory part of the scheme, it was unfortunate that so much time was wasted in searching for the fisherman who it was originally thought might operate the scheme, as it meant that we were working against time in the latter stages. This seems to point to the fact that it is usually impracticable to nominate from the UK a certain man in Norway for a task, but preferable to leave matters to the ingenuity of the local organisations on the spot.

'2.   The fact that the Lark organisation was off the air for a long period was a considerable handicap. It will probably be agreed that W/T arrangements generally are far from satisfactory, and no effort should be spared to improve these.

'3.   Pending a report from the engineer who is still in hospital suffering from frostbite, it is impossible to say whether the defects in the motor experienced during the trip were due to lack of foresight, but the actual timing of the operation was thrown out owing to this. This will have affected the escape arrangements made by the Lark organisation, but as events transpired, they did not come into the picture.

'4.   The failure of the towing arrangements, resulting in the chariots breaking away in the heavy weather experienced actually inside the fjord was a disaster which defeated the whole enterprise, but it is a technical matter which lies outside the scope of this report. All concerned ascribe the highest possible praise to the skipper of the boat for his conduct throughout.

'5.   The failure to sink the boat [*Arthur*] seems inexplicable. I am not clear at what stage it was decided to drop the idea of scuttling charges, which were clearly envisaged in the scheme as originally propounded to us. It is obvious that whatever method was to be adopted, no uncertainty should have been allowed to exist as to the complete disappearance of the boat.

'6.   It was unfortunate that the diving suits were not jettisoned before the boat was abandoned, as it is possible that the Germans might have assumed it was merely a gun-running expedition had they not been found. All the ship's papers were removed and buried ashore, but there seems an element of uncertainty as to whether a chart of the Shetlands was destroyed. This point can doubtless be cleared up.

'7.   A criticism seems to have been made by one of the Norwegians as to the size of the maps provided for the escape, but all the other members of the party seem to agree they were adequate. The food arrangements for the escape seem to have been good.

'8.   Co-operation between the British and Norwegian members of the party seems to have been first class, and every man [appears] to have pulled his weight and more. It is only a tragedy that an operation which contained so many elements of success should have failed in its main object, but this cannot be ascribed to any failure on the part of the individuals concerned. While it is not for us to judge technical matters, it would otherwise seem that the failure is in large measure due to the inadequate trial and testing of chariots and towing gear in all weathers and under all conditions, and that a needless risk was taken in jeopardising a first class plan through insufficient attention to testing beforehand.'

There is little doubt the report would have been seen by Commanders Sladen and Fell, and, through them, its contents made known to their teams, both British and Norwegian, at Scalloway. It can only be imagined how difficult it would have been for all concerned to read and accept the summary of that last sentence considering the months of hard work that had gone into making the mission a success. In reality, the cause of the mission having to be abandoned was the failure of the bolts connecting the chariots to their cables to withstand the strain placed on them in the extreme conditions encountered. Could those extreme conditions have been replicated by testing beforehand, as suggested? The author believes this to be most unlikely.

Awards for their part in Operation Title

Leif Larsen was awarded the Conspicuous Gallantry Medal, the first time it had been awarded to a non-British national. A comprehensive collection of Larsen's war medals, including his CGM, is held on display at Nordsjøfartmuseet, Telavåg, Bergen. Sub Lieutenant 'Jock' Brewster received the Distinguished Service Cross, and *Arthur*'s engineer, P.O. Bjørnøy, was awarded the Distinguished Service Medal. The other five RN divers Craig, Brown, Causer, Tebb and Evans were mentioned in despatches, as were the other two Norwegian members of *Arthur*'s crew, Strand and Kalve.

Bill Moore from Scalloway Museum reports that Tebb's daughter, 'Rocky', donated her father's Mentioned in Despatches Certificate to the museum.

Craig's medals and memorabilia came to auction recently and were acquired by Michael Beckett, a keen collector of commando-related items. Michael has kindly given permission for Craig's MiD Certificate to be reproduced herein.

By the KING'S Order the name of
Sergeant Donald Craig,
Royal Engineers,
was placed on record on
28 January, 1943,
as mentioned in a Despatch for distinguished service.
I am charged to express
His Majesty's high appreciation.

First Lord of the Admiralty

Chapter 16

Robert Paul Evans – A Mother's Son

In 1964, the West German government agreed to provide £1 million in financial compensation to British victims of National Socialism. The distribution of the money, organized by the British Foreign Office, turned into a major public scandal as a number of British PoWs – among them survivors of the 'Great Escape' – had their claims rejected. The refusal of several British PoWs to accept their exclusion from the scheme led to a parliamentary inquiry into what became known as 'The Sachsenhausen Affair' in 1967. Given that provisions of the agreement with West Germany had precluded indemnification to mistreated PoWs, the distribution of the money almost inevitably led to bitterness and discontent.

FO 950/3010 – Nazi Persecution Claim under the Anglo-German Agreement 1964
Mrs Rose Evans for Robert Paul Evans (deceased)

This file in the National Archives, Kew, is a slim one, with what little correspondence there is leaving questions unanswered. From it, we see that Mrs Rose Evans received a letter from the Foreign Office, dated 21 May 1965:

'Ref HNP/2181

'Madam

'I am directed by Mr Secretary Stewart to inform you that your application of the 11th May 1955 [*sic*] to participate in the compensation payable under the terms of the Anglo-German Agreement dated the 9th June 1964, in respect of United Kingdom nationals who were victim of National Socialist measures of persecution, has been registered.

'I am, however, to draw your attention to Paragraph 3 of the Notes for Guidance and to emphasise that no payment can be made until after the period for registration has ended on the 31st July 1965 and all claims have been received, when a further communication will be sent to you. Until then no action on your part is necessary except to keep this Department informed of any change in your address.

'I am, Madam, your obedient servant.'

A second letter to Mrs Rose Evans from the Foreign Office was dated 13 August 1965:

'Ref HNP/2181

'Dear Madam

'In this Department's letter of 21st May 1965 notifying you of registration of an application for compensation for persecution by the Nazis of the late R.P. Evans you were informed that no payment could be made until after 31st July 1965.

'I am pleased to inform you that a grant to you has been approved of £1,000-0-00 and a payable order for this amount will be sent to you under separate cover in the course of the next few days.

'Yours faithfully, E.A.S. Brooks'

A handwritten letter, dated 28 August 1965, was sent from 33 Foxley Road, Brixton, to the Foreign Office, Ref No 11800:

'Dear Sirs
'Re 2181 Compensation
'For Nazi Persecution
'I have much pleasure in acknowledging your cheque for £1,000 for which I am most grateful.
'I am, Yours faithfully
'R C Evans'

A second handwritten letter, dated 11 November 1966, was sent from 33 Foxley Road, Brixton, to the Foreign Office:

'I wish to acknowledge your further cheque paid in full settlement in respect of Nazi War Victims.
'My most grateful appreciation.
'I am yours faithfully
'R C Evans'

Mrs Evans obviously had someone write the above two letters on her behalf, as the writing differs from her shaky signature. For what amount was the second cheque that Mrs Evans acknowledged? In the file in the National Archives is a brief note:

'F.O. File Note 11 Nov. R P Evans
'One death grant paid
'£2,993-15-00'

From the above, it is difficult to make out whether this figure included or was in addition to the original £1,000 payment. The 2024 equivalent of £1,000 in 1966 is around £17,430; the equivalent of £2,993 is £39,967. In 1960, the average UK house price was £2,530.

For Mrs Rose Evans, by then 86 years old and widowed six years earlier, this was but another official acknowledgement that her son had been executed by the Nazis. The financial compensation would have been of little consolation for the two years she had lived in the vain hope of hearing that her missing son was safe and well, and for the rest of her long life to mourn his death. Mrs Evans died four years later, on 2 April 1970, aged 90.

Author's Note

In my efforts to trace family members of Bob Evans, I contacted the *Brixton Blog and Bugle*, which in April 2022 kindly posted an article headed 'Tragic story of a Brixton war hero'. As a direct result of this, in July 2022, I was contacted by Patrick and Jane

Scully, who helpfully provided sufficient information to enable me to construct the family tree. From this, it will be seen that Jane Scully (née Evans) is the niece of Bob Evans. Jane tells me that her father, Ralph, spoke little of the war or of the death of his younger brother, Bob. Unfortunately, it seems that no papers relating to Bob's war service have survived within the family, not even his Mentioned in Despatches Certificate. It set me to wondering if Ralph or his parents were ever able to visit Bob's grave in Oslo. The inscription below the cross on the gravestone there reads:

'HOW STRANGELY
HIGH ENDEAVOUR MAY BE BLEST
WHEN PIETY AND VALOUR
JOINTLY GO'

Chapter 17

Called to Account

O fficially named the International Military Tribunal (IMT), the Nuremberg Trials were held by the Allies against representatives of the defeated Nazi Germany, for plotting and carrying out invasions of other countries, and other crimes, during the Second World War. Proposals for how to punish the defeated Nazi leaders ranged from a show trial (the Soviet Union's preferred option) to summary executions (backed by the United Kingdom). In mid-1945, France, the Soviet Union, the United Kingdom and the United States agreed to convene a joint tribunal in Nuremberg scene of Hitler's stage-managed Nazi Party rallies from the early 1920s until the outbreak of war with the Nuremberg Charter as its legal instrument. Between 20 November 1945 and 1 October 1946, the IMT tried twenty-one of the most important surviving political, military and economic leaders of Nazi Germany, as well as leaders of six German organizations. Most of the defendants were charged with war crimes and crimes against humanity.

Names of British soldiers, sailors and marines murdered by the Germans after being captured while engaged in commando operations were given in an official report placed before the tribunal. The report was given by Mr G.D. Roberts, KC, one of the British prosecutors, as part of the case against Wilhelm Keitel, former Chief of the German High Command, and Alfred

Jodl, former Chief of the Operations Staff. It set out how the German armed forces under their command carried out Hitler's order of 1942 that allied commandos must be slaughtered to the last man. One example given concerned an abortive attempt to attack the German battleship *Tirpitz* with human torpedoes in Trondheim Fjord in October 1942. The report stated, 'Only the British seaman Robert Paul Evans born January 14th 1922 in London could be arrested, the others escaping into Sweden. Violence representing a breach of International law could not be proved against him. In accordance, however, with the Führer's order, he was shot on the 19th January, 1943.'

Wilhelm Bodewin Johann Gustav Keitel (22 September 1882 – 16 October 1946) was a German field marshal and war criminal who held office as chief of the Oberkommando der Wehrmacht (OKW), the high command of Nazi Germany's armed forces, during the Second World War. In that capacity, Keitel signed a number of criminal orders and directives that led to numerous war crimes. Keitel's rise to the Wehrmacht's high command began with his appointment as the head of the Armed Forces Office at the Reich Ministry of War in 1935. Having taken command of the Wehrmacht in 1938, Hitler replaced the ministry with the OKW and Keitel became its chief. He was reviled among his military colleagues as Hitler's habitual 'yes-man'. After the war, Keitel was indicted by the IMT as one of the 'major war criminals'. He was found guilty on all counts of the indictment: crimes against humanity, crimes against peace, criminal conspiracy and war crimes. He was sentenced to death and executed by hanging in Nuremburg on 16 October 1946.

Alfred Josef Ferdinand Jodl (10 May 1890 – 16 October 1946) was a German Generaloberst who served as the Chief of the Operations Staff of the OKW throughout the Second World War. After the war, Jodl was indicted by the IMT on charges of conspiracy to commit crimes against peace, planning, initiating and waging wars of aggression, war crimes and crimes against humanity. The principal charges against him related to his signature of the criminal Commando and Commissar Orders. Found guilty on all charges, he was sentenced to death and executed by hanging in Nuremberg on 16 October 1946.

Paul Nikolaus von Falkenhorst (17 January 1885 – 18 June 1968) was a German national and Generaloberst in the German Army during Second World War. He planned and commanded the German invasion of Norway in 1940, and was commander of German troops during the occupation from 1940–44. Between 29 July and 2 August 1946, von Falkenhorst was tried for war crimes in Brunswick, Norway, before a joint British and Norwegian Military Court sitting with a Judge Advocate. He had passed on the Führerbefehl, the Commando Order, which required captured commandos to be shot. The evidence at trial included Falkenhorst's order that commandos, if kept alive for interrogation, should not 'survive for more than twenty-four hours'. He distributed the order in 1942, reminding his subordinates of it in 1943, insisting that the captured commandos be handed over to the SD, the intelligence service of the SS, for execution.

At the Nuremburg Trials two months earlier, during the questioning of Rear Admiral Gerhard Wagner, chief of staff (Operations) of Naval Warfare Command (Seekriegsleitung), it was revealed that when Evans was captured, he was interviewed directly by von Falkenhorst. Von Falkenhorst faced nine charges, the fifth of which read:

> 'Committing a War Crime in that he in the Kingdom of Norway, in or about the month of January, 1943, in violation of the laws and usages of war, was responsible as Commander-in-Chief of the Armed Forces, Norway (Wehrmachtbefehlshaber Norwegen), for the handing over by forces under his command, to the Sicherheitsdienst (Security Service) of Seaman Robert Evans, a British Prisoner of War who had taken part in Commando Operations with the result that the said Seaman Robert Evans was killed.'

To this and the other nine charges von Falkenhorst pleaded 'Not guilty', his defence arguing that he was acting under superior orders. The prosecution withdrew the fifth charge relating to Seaman Robert Evans during the course of the trial, apparently on the ground that at no time was this prisoner of war in the custody of the German armed forces but was an SD prisoner from the beginning. The accused was also acquitted on one of the other charges, but on all other charges he was found guilty and sentenced to death. However, on appeal, this was commuted to twenty years' imprisonment. Falkenhorst was released from prison in 1953 due to bad health and died in 1968 following a heart attack.

Gerhard Friedrich Ernst Flesch (8 October 1909 – 28 February 1948) was born in Posen, Germany, and by 1933 had become a member of the NSDAP (Nationalsozialistische Deutsche Arbeiterpartei, the Nazi Party). In 1934, he obtained a law degree, and by 1936 was a member of the Gestapo, whose chief, Reinhard Heydrich, appointed him head of a unit to control the religious sects of Germany.

In April 1940, when he was assigned to Norway, Flesch's first job was Kommandeur of the SiPo and SD in Bergen. On 11 October 1941, he was appointed Kommandeur of the Sicherheitspolizei and the Sicherheitsdienst in Trondheim. As Kommandeur of the district, he was also in overall command of Falstad concentration camp outside Trondheim and the prisons in Trondheim. He was promoted to the rank of Obersturmbannführer (lieutenant colonel) and received the title of Oberregierungsrat (senior government councillor). His immediate superior was Heinrich Fehlis. On 8 May 1945, he fled from Trondheim with a gold bar in his luggage. He was caught and sent back with a police escort on a train, from which he made an unsuccessful attempt to escape.

Flesch, a notorious torturer, ordered the execution of many members of the Norwegian resistance movement without any trial. In 1946, he was tried for various cases of torture and murder and with a series of war crimes committed in Norway; seven instances of ordering the murders of a total of thirty-seven prisoners, albeit four of those targeted were not killed, five instances of torture (*verschärfte Vernehmung*, 'enhanced interrogation') and one instance of withholding medical treatment, resulting in death. Flesch was found guilty of ordering twenty-five murders, twenty-one of which were carried out, all counts of torture, and the withholding of medical treatment.

It was Flesch who gave the order to shoot the six English prisoners held at Grini. He maintained that he had been told by his superior, Heinrich Fehlis, that all six had been sentenced to death by a *Standgericht* (court martial). These were not sentences as such but merely decisions taken by Fehlis, who admitted that the shooting of these six men was an act of reprisal camouflaged as a *Standgericht* sentence.

Flesch was sentenced to death by firing squad. He appealed to the Supreme Court of Norway on procedural grounds and on the contention that his sentence was too harsh. However, his appeal was rejected on 12 February 1948, and at midnight on 28 February, the sentence was carried out at Kristiansten fortress, where many loyal Norwegians had previously perished on his direct orders.

Heinrich Fehlis (1 November 1906 – May 1945) was a German Schutzstaffel (SS) officer during the Second World War and commanded the SiPo and the SD during the German occupation of Norway. A newly educated attorney when Hitler rose to power in 1933, he joined the SA (Sturmabteilung, the original paramilitary wing of the Nazis) that year on 1 April and the Nazi Party on 1 May. On 10 September 1935, Fehlis joined the SS, where he successfully applied to work for the Gestapo in Berlin. On 21 April 1940, Fehlis became leader of the Einsatzkommando (mobile killing squad) in Oslo, and in November that year he succeeded to the dual command of the SD and SiPo in Norway. He rose to the ranks of SS-Standartenführer and, in June 1944, SS-Oberführer.

Together with his subordinate, Hellmuth Reinhard, Fehlis regulated the use of torture and sentenced prisoners to death in so-called 'office judgements'. Following the German surrender on 8 May 1945, Fehlis and other SS officials attempted to escape capture by members of Milorg, the official Norwegian resistance network. He arranged for Gestapo members to be hidden among ordinary soldiers in the Wehrmacht, personally leading a force of around seventy-five men disguised in Gebirgskorps Norwegen (German Mountain Corps) uniforms to a military camp near Porsgrunn. Following a tip-off, the camp fell under suspicion and was surrounded. During negotiations, Fehlis (who impersonated a lieutenant named Gerstheuer) requested an hour to prepare for surrender. Milorg agreed, but when they finally entered the camp, it was in a disorderly condition with many of the Germans in a state of intoxication. Fehlis' body was discovered in one of the camp rooms; he had found the means to first poison and then shoot himself, saving himself from a war crimes trial and probable execution.

Oscar Hans (born 6 February 1910 in Germany; date of death unknown) was an officer of the German SS-Sonderkommando during the occupation of Norway who led the execution of more than 300 prisoners, including 195 killed at Trandumskogen. After the war, he was initially sentenced to death by the Supreme Court of Norway, but successfully appealed against his sentence and was expelled from the country. He was later brought to trial before a British Military Court in Hamburg, and on 22 August 1948 was sentenced to fifteen years' imprisonment for the execution of six British citizens. He was released in April 1954.

Møller (first name unknown), Naval Commandant at Trondheim Fjord. His name is mentioned in a note on file ADM 358/2129 at the National Archives, Kew, which makes interesting reading but leaves the reader wondering who 'Bischoff' was:

'DISTRIKSTCOMMAND
'1 TRØNDELAG   Trondheim

'Bischoff well remembered the arrest of Seaman Evans who was wounded in a brush with a frontier patrol while trying to get to Sweden. He was examined at Misjonshotellet (Gestapo HQ) and at first refused any information regarding his mission but was then confronted with the diving suit which had been retrieved in the neighbourhood of the vessel which had been sunk. The suspicions of the Gestapo had been aroused by both incidents occurring simultaneously. Evans had made a good impression and been regarded as a military prisoner of war and was handed over to the Wehrmacht to be sent to Berlin after 3 or 4 days. [*]

'On being questioned as to how the vessel had got through the controls Evans had stated that it was challenged by a German patrol boat which merely asked whether they had any eggs on board and when they replied in the negative had made no inspection. This had been referred to later in the enquiry which the German authorities held on the incident and in consequence thereof the Naval Commandant, Møller had committed suicide.'

[*As we later discovered, this did not happen. Evans was handed over to the SD, the intelligence branch of the SS, and sent to Grini Prison, Oslo, arriving there on 14 December 1942, five weeks after his capture and hospital treatment.]

Reichskommissar **Josef Terboven** was responsible for the Telavåg reprisals of April 1942 [see Notes] and many other violent acts of repression and crimes against humanity in German occupied Norway. There is little doubt that, upon standing trial post-war, Terboven would have been found guilty and sentenced to death by hanging. However, with the announcement of the German surrender, Terboven retreated to a bunker where he blew himself up with 50kg of dynamite.

Chapter 18

Operation Source – A Question

With the failure of Operation Title to tame 'The Beast' and *Tirpitz* continuing to pose a threat to Allied shipping, much thought was given to ways and means of finishing off the German battleship once and for all. Subsequent to the development of the chariot, the evolution of underwater warfare had, during the early part of 1943, resulted in the design and building of four-man midget submarines known as X-Craft, which, it was considered, might stand a chance of success where the chariots had failed. And so, Operation Source was launched, of which the following citation records the result:

'ADMIRALTY.
'*Whitehall. 22nd February, 1944.*

'The KING has been graciously pleased to approve the award of the VICTORIA CROSS for valour to:

'Lieutenant Basil Charles Godfrey Place, D.S.C., Royal Navy.

'Lieutenant Donald Cameron, R.N.R.

'Lieutenants Place and Cameron were the Commanding Officers of two of His Majesty's Midget Submarines X 7 and X 6 which on 22nd September 1943 carried out a most daring and successful attack on the German Battleship Tirpitz, moored in the protected anchorage of Kaafjord, North Norway.

'To reach the anchorage necessitated the penetration of an enemy minefield and a passage of fifty miles up the fiord, known to be vigilantly patrolled by the enemy and to be guarded by nets, gun defences and listening posts, this after a passage of at least a thousand miles from base.

'Having successfully eluded all these hazards and entered the fleet anchorage, Lieutenants Place and Cameron, with a complete disregard for danger, worked their small craft past the close anti-submarine and torpedo nets surrounding the Tirpitz, and from a position inside these nets, carried out a cool and determined attack.

'Whilst they were still inside the nets a fierce enemy counter attack by guns and depth charges developed which made their withdrawal impossible. Lieutenants Place and Cameron therefore scuttled their craft to prevent them falling into the hands of the enemy. Before doing so they took every measure to ensure the safety of their crews, the majority of whom, together with themselves, were subsequently taken prisoner.

'In the course of the operation these very small craft pressed home their attack to the full, in doing so accepting all the dangers inherent in such vessels and facing every possible hazard which ingenuity could devise for the protection in harbour of vitally important Capital Ships.

'The courage, endurance and utter contempt for danger in the immediate face of the enemy shown by Lieutenants Place and Cameron during this determined and successful attack were supreme.'

Cameron and Place survived the mission, as did four other members. Engine Room Artificer Edmund Goddard was awarded the Conspicuous Gallantry Medal, while Sub Lieutenants Robert Aitken, Richard Haddon Kendal and John Thornton Lorimer each received a DSO. Following their capture, Lieutenants Cameron and Place spent the remainder of the war as prisoners in Marlag 'O', a prisoner-of-war camp at Westertimke, near Bremen, reserved specifically to hold Royal Navy officers. While there, they had their portraits painted by a fellow prisoner and official war artist, John Worsley, who later became President of the Royal Society of Marine Artists. The portraits, painted on the back of some curtain material from the prisoners' hut, now hang in the National Maritime Museum, Greenwich.

And now to the question which continues to puzzle the author. Lieutenants Cameron and Place, through their highly successful commando-style mission, caused such damage to *Tirpitz* as to put it out of action for some considerable time. Upon being captured, they were merely held prisoner by the

Germans until the war ended. Why, then, was Able Seaman R.P. Evans, captured after an unsuccessful mission that failed to reach the same target let alone cause any damage to it executed?

It is a fact that seafarers the world over in merchant ships and warships alike have, historically, tended to look out for each other. The author would like to believe that the officers of *Tirpitz*, with a grudging admiration for what had been achieved and wishing to ensure that these brave naval officers and men did not fall into the hands of the SD or the SS, arranged for them to be sent quickly and directly to Marlag 'O'.

It is a strange thing, war.

Chapter 19

Tirpitz

On 15 September 1944, a force of twenty-seven RAF Lancaster bombers, operating from Russia, dropped a series of enormous 6-tonne Tallboy bombs on *Tirpitz*. Despite the hindrance of a smokescreen, one Tallboy hit *Tirpitz* on the foredeck just behind the bow, causing extensive damage. A report from an SIS agent in Norway stated:

'Damage is as follows. She got a direct hit on the starboard side which made a hole from the bow towards the stern seventeen metres along. The hole is both above and below the waterline and is so large that motorboats could go in. Neither the turrets nor forepart of the ship is under water, neither have they been under water, but just after the attack the ship had a list to starboard and the forepart of the ship was low in the water. How much it was difficult to see because of the fog [from fires and smoke generators]. Ship is now on an even keel but is still down by the head.'

Tirpitz was patched up and limped out of the Altafjord and down to an anchorage at Håkøya, an island close to Tromsø. Once there, the ship was again within the range of Lancasters operating from Britain. Indeed, it was attacked by Lancasters from Nos 9 and 617 Squadrons on 29 October, but low cloud over the target hampered their efforts. The ship was not hit directly, but a near miss damaged one of the engines and caused some flooding. A further attack was made on 12 November by aircraft from the same squadrons; this time the weather was fine and clear, German ground defences were not prepared and the smokescreen units had not been moved to the ship's new location in time. In addition, the German fighter protection aircraft were slow to respond to the warning that another attack was on its way, thus giving the Lancasters the time they required to make their approach without interference. They achieved several direct hits and near misses, causing *Tirpitz* to capsize – 971 German sailors were killed, roughly half the ship's complement. To Churchill's delight and satisfaction, 'The Beast' had finally been tamed.

On Saturday, 13 August 2022, *The Times* published an obituary for Sydney Grimes, wireless operator of one of the Lancasters that sank the *Tirpitz*. It carried the following account:

'Grimes had first flown against the *Tirpitz* during an unsuccessful raid on October 29, 1944. Two weeks later the squadron was sent back. The mission was codenamed Operation Catechism. The squadron's Lancasters were modified, with their mid-upper turrets removed to reduce the weight of each aircraft and extend their range for the 2,200-mile round trip from airfields in northern Scotland. Each aircraft carried a single 12,000lb "Tallboy" bomb, which was capable of piercing the *Tirpitz*'s armour.

'According to the squadron's operations book, Grimes's Lancaster, one of 18 aircraft from 617 Squadron, took off at 3.19am. They flew past the Shetland Islands, crossed the Norwegian coast-line in the far north at low level and then turned south over Sweden, ignoring its neutrality, and approached Tromsø from the east. The German defences were taken by surprise; no fighters were seen.

'Grimes had his own reason for wanting to see the destruction of the battleship. He told John Nichol, author of *Return of the Dambusters*, "My brother was in the navy on HMS *London*, escorting Arctic convoys. He'd told me about the *Tirpitz* and I knew it worried him, so I thought if I could do something to help him out, all the better."

'At 8.43am, Grimes watched as his Lancaster, flown by New Zealander, Flight Lieutenant Barney Gumbley, bombed the target from 15,400ft. Their Tallboy hit the sea about 20 yards from *Tirpitz* and a dull red glow was seen forward of the port bow. It was one of several bombs that fell close to the battleship. Two aircraft scored direct hits. "Bombing by 617 was," says the operations book, "concentrated and accurate." At 8.51am there was an enormous explosion as an ammunition store on the ship exploded and *Tirpitz* capsized.

'Grimes recalled a great cheer when they heard that *Tirpitz* had been destroyed. "But the biggest emotion was a sense of relief that we wouldn't have to go back again," he said. When the crews returned home they were greeted as heroes. They were sent to London for a ceremonial visit during which they were congratulated by Sir Archibald Sinclair, the Air Minister. "There was plenty of congratulations and back-slapping," Grimes said in his interview with Nicol, "but the best thing was that after his speech, Sinclair gave us 48 hours leave." The minister's announcement allowed Grimes to get home for his wife's 21st birthday.'

Sydney Grimes, wartime wireless operator who completed forty-one missions with Bomber Command, was born on 6 May 1922, three months after Able Seaman Robert Paul Evans. He died on 27 May 2022, aged 100.

Notes

1. Akershus Fortress, Oslo.

The Fortress became a prison during the Nazi occupation. Never successfully captured since being built in 1308, it was surrendered without a shot being fired when the Norwegian government evacuated the capital in 1940. The Fortress was liberated on 11th May 1945 when it was handed over to Terje Rollem, in his capacity as an officer of Milorg, the Norwegian Resistance Movement. During the war several prisoners were executed there. After the war, eight Norwegian traitors who had been tried for war crimes and sentenced to death were executed there.

2. *Arthur*, Norwegian Motor Fishing Vessel

Built around 1898 on Godøy, an island off the west coast of Norway, *Arthur* was clinker built as a fishing boat designed for sail, being later modified several times. In 1934 at Vik, Tomrefjord she was lengthened by 10 ft (3 m) having her stern replaced with a taller one. In 1938 at Frøstad boatyard, also in Tomrefjord she was lengthened again and had a 50-hp Norwegian Brunvold two-cylinder semi-diesel engine installed. In October 1941, Larsen was part of the crew of the Norwegian fishing vessel, *Nordsjöen* which had been used as a mine-layer off the coast of Norway. She sank in a storm and Larsen, after an epic struggle against all odds, reached the village of Soviksnes where he found *Arthur*, a typical Norwegian fishing boat, at anchor and un-manned. With a small party of fellow-Norwegians, Larsen boarded the vessel during the night, slipped anchor and sailed *Arthur* across the North Sea to Lunna Voe. She was to provide valuable service as part of the Shetland Bus up to and including Operation Title one year later. Scuttled in 1942 after the failed mission, *Arthur* was raised by the Germans who made yet more alterations to her in order to use her for transporting prisoners. This fact that became known after the war, when the new owners, finding a scrap of wood hidden in the boat with a name on it, were able to trace that person, a former prisoner in a Norwegian concentration camp. Shortly after the war ended, *Arthur* was again modified, this time for herring fishing around the Shetlands and Faeroes. However, by the early 1980's she had reached that state in her long life when she failed to qualify for the renewal of her sailing certificate. The cost of bringing her up to the required standard was not an economical proposition and she sank to obscurity in Moldefjord in 1982. Rumours of *Arthur* being salvaged float around but it is doubtful if she herself will ever float again.

3. ASHBOURNE, Lord Edward Russell Gibson, Vice-Admiral CB DSO (1901 – 1983)

A submarine specialist who had a distinguished career in WWII during which he took part in the Sicily landings and was the first British naval officer to command a task group covering an American amphibious operation – 1944 US assault on the island of Pegun (Mapia). In 1930 he commanded submarine H48 and in 1934, HM Submarine *Pandora*. Early in 1940 he became chief staff officer to Flag Officer (Submarines) and continued in the submarine service on the experimental staff. Further sea service and Admiralty shore appointments saw him finally Flag Officer and Admiral Superintendent at Gibraltar.

4. Brendmo Farm

It is possible that the Norwegian resistance organisation, Lark, planned a reprisal against Brendmo Farm, and Mrs Brendmo in particular, for her part in alerting the authorities to Larsen and his party during their escape to Sweden. The following extract is from a report dated 8th November, 1942, made by Otto Arne Hansen of Vikhammer, a member of Lark. While this slightly pre-dates the Brendmo incident, it reveals that such reprisals were not uncommon.

'On 3rd October I met Sörli* and a friend of his in Trondheim and was told to travel to Verdalen to set fire to a farm there. The idea was actually to take a boat to Verdal and cycle further up the valley, but then I was afraid of being recognised (retaliated against) in Trondheim, so I decided to walk up instead. I thought I could do this in 9-10 days. I started on the 7th. Walked round Mostadmarka, Hegra and Fortradalen where I left my rucksack in a safe place and went on the 11th over to Verdalen. I came to a bridge over the river near Sul around midnight and walked along the road further to orientate myself, when I was stopped by a German patrol of two men who demanded my ID card and border passport. They searched me and then found the material that I had brought with me to use at work (arson.) I was then taken to their quarters a little further up, and I explained that I was once working on the farm as a schoolboy and I intended to burn the farm as revenge for a prejudicial act I thought I had been exposed to. The Germans then called for a car that arrived a couple of hours later. It was a small 4-seater Opel, and three men and the driver came with me down the valley. Before it was light in the morning we arrived at a large building, probably near Stiklestad. I was treated relatively nicely, and the German officer who interrogated me seemed to believe my explanation.'

This report comes from File [NHM] SOE/22/3/1 Box 35a, Norway Resistance Museum, Oslo by courtesy of Ivar Kraglund, Director.

Translated from the original Norwegian using Google Translate.

*Odd Sørlie was the SOE contact in Trondheim

5. 154 Chiltern Court, London

Chiltern Court, Baker Street, London, is a large block of flats at the street's northern end, facing Regent's Park and Marylebone Road. It was built between 1927 and 1929 above the Baker Street tube station by the Metropolitan Railway. Originally intended as a hotel and as its company headquarters, and begun in 1912, the Metropolitan's plans were interrupted by the First World War. When construction recommenced in the late 1920s, the building was redesigned as a block of flats and the Chiltern Court Restaurant. The architect was Charles Walter Clark. During the 1930s the block was home to a number of notable figures, including the writers H. G. Wells, who held a weekly literary salon at his apartment, and Arnold Bennett, who died at the court in 1931. The composer Eric Coates lived in the block between 1930 and 1936, and the cartoonist David Low was also a resident. During World War II, the Special Operations Executive was based at 64 Baker Street, and its Scandinavian Section was located in three flats at Chiltern Court, from where it directed operations including Title and Freshman.

6. CUNNINGHAM, Admiral of the Fleet **Andrew Browne Cunningham, 1st Viscount Cunningham of Hyndhope,** KT, GCB, OM, DSO & Two Bars was widely known throughout the Royal Navy and beyond as 'ABC.'

Admiral Cunningham [1883 – 1963] born in Rathmines, Dublin, entered the Royal Navy in 1897 as a naval cadet in the officers' training ship *Britannia*, passing out in 1898. He commanded a destroyer in the First World War and through most of the interwar years during which he was awarded the Distinguished Service Order and two Bars for his actions in the Dardanelles and the Baltic.

Cunningham was made Commander-in-Chief, Mediterranean, hoisting his flag in HMS Warspite on 6th June 1939 and in this capacity he led British naval forces to victory in several critical Mediterranean naval battles namely the attack on Taranto in 1940 and the Battle of Cape Matapan in 1941. Cunningham controlled the defence of the Mediterranean supply lines through Alexandria, Gibraltar, and the key chokepoint of Malta. He also directed naval support for various major Allied landings in the Western Mediterranean. In autumn 1943 Cunningham was promoted to First Sea Lord, the professional head of the Royal Navy, a position he held until his retirement in 1946. He was ennobled as Baron Cunningham of Hyndhope in 1945 and made Viscount Cunningham of Hyndhope the following year.

7. Robert Paul EVANS - Family Tree

Ralph George
Evans
(b. 1882 d. 1960)

Rose Catherine
(née Smith)
(b. 1880 – d. 2nd April 1970)

Married 6th July 1916

Richard <u>Ralph</u>
(b. 15th November 1919
(d. 19th December 1989)

<u>Robert</u> Paul
(b. 14th January 1922)
(d. 19th January 1943)

First Married (1948)
Jeanette Barbyer

Susan   Michael

Second   Married

Sybil Ann Scott

Jane Catherine   Simon   Karen

Married

Patrick Scully

In the 1921 Census, Ralph and Rose Evans were living with their two year old son, Ralph Jnr., at 315 Camberwell Road, Camberwell. By 1939 they had moved one mile away to 125

Vassall Road. At some later date they moved just around the corner to 33 Foxley Road.

8. FELL, William Richmond 'Tiny' CMG, CBE, DSC

Fell was born in Wellington, New Zealand 31st January, 1897, and was educated at Wellington College, NZ, before attending Crediton Grammar School, Devon and the Royal Naval Engineering College, Keyham. He entered the Royal Navy on 15th April, 1916 and served in HMS *Warspite* 1916 – 1917, seeing action at the Battle of Jutland. By November 1924 he was First Lieutenant in HM Submarine K2 then L16, both of the 1st Submarine Flotilla, Atlantic Fleet. After passing the Submarine Commanding Officer's Qualifying Course (COQC) in HMS *Alecto* in November 1927 he was appointed to Commanding Officer of HM Submarine H31 of the 5th Submarine Flotilla, Portsmouth then served in various other submarines and surface ships including the submarine depot ships HMS *Alecto, Titania* and *Dolphin*. His experience and ability as an instructor saw Fell appointed Teacher/Commanding Officer of the COQC, colloquially known as the Perisher course, between 1930 – 1932 and again 1935 – 1937, one of only three officers to serve in this capacity twice. September 1939 saw Fell in command of the submarine reserve fleet at Portland until, in April, 1940 he commanded a group of five trawlers, known as the Gubbins Flotilla, which was despatched to support soldiers landed in Norway under Colonel Gubbins. For this Fell was awarded the DSC. He was mentioned in despatches for his action while in command of the infantry landing ship, HMS *Prince Charles* when taking part in Operation Archery, the raid on Vågsøy, December 1941. In 1942 he was selected by Admiral Sir Max Horton to set up a training base in Western Scotland where equipment and men were prepared for the human torpedoes or 'chariots' that took part in Operation Title and later, the X-Craft for Operation Source. Fell was appointed CBE for his service as Commanding Officer HMS *Bonaventure*, depot ship for midget submarines in home waters, Loch Striven and the Pacific. After the war he served as Boom Defence Officer and Salvage Officer in Malta, Portsmouth and the Clyde until, in 1957, he was appointed CMG for his role as Principal Salvage Officer, Suez. Fell's book, 'The Sea Surrenders' recounts his efforts in this respect. Upon his retirement, Fell returned to his native New Zealand and died there at Eastbourne, Wellington on 28th November 1981.

9. HMS *Daedalus*

Royal Naval Air Station Lee-on-Solent, (RNAS Lee-on-Solent; or HMS *Daedalus* 1939 - 1959 is a former Royal Naval Air Station located near Lee-on-the-Solent in Hampshire, approximately 4 miles (6.44 km) west of Portsmouth, on the coast of the Solent. It was one of the primary shore airfields of the Fleet Air Arm and was first established as a seaplane base in 1917 during the First World War. The aerodrome opened in 1934 and was commissioned as HMS *Daedalus* on 24 May 1939, the day administrative control of the Fleet Air Arm was transferred to the Admiralty from the Royal Air Force. During the Second World War it was home to the office of the Admiral (Air) and was the main depot for Naval Air Ratings.

10. HMS *Dolphin*

The seventeenth Royal Navy vessel to be named HMS *Dolphin* was the Royal Navy shore establishment sited at Fort Blockhouse in Gosport. HMS *Dolphin* was the home of the Royal Navy Submarine Service from 1904 to 1999 and the location of the Royal Navy Submarine School.

11. HMS *Drake*

The main naval barracks at Devonport and a Royal Navy accounting base, HMS *Drake* appears on sailors' records as their home base. They may not physically have been at Devonport between the dates shown as, any time they are not allocated to another ship's crew, they revert to HMS *Drake*. This may happen while they are in port awaiting their next ship, or in transit in another ship but not part of that ship's crew.

12. HMS *Raleigh*

A stone frigate (shore establishment), serving as the basic training facility of the Royal Navy at Torpoint, Cornwall, United Kingdom. It is spread over several square miles, and has damage control simulators and fire-fighting training facilities, as well as a permanently moored training ship, the former HMS *Brecon*. Its principal function is the delivery of both New Entry Training & Basic Training. HMS *Raleigh* was commissioned on 9 January 1940 as a training establishment for Ordinary Seamen following the Military Training Act which required that all males aged 20 and 21 years old be called up for six months full–time military training, and then transferred to the reserve.

13. HMS St Vincent

A shore establishment of the Royal Navy, located in Gosport. The name was given to the Forton Barracks site in Gosport in 1927, after the training establishment that been set up aboard the old first rate HMS St Vincent in 1862. The new HMS St Vincent was commissioned on 1 June 1927, originally like its predecessor as a training establishment for boys and juniors. On the outbreak of the Second World War, the boys were evacuated to the Isle of Man, where they merged with those evacuated from HMS Caledonia to form HMS St George, which was formally established in 1939. HMS St Vincent meanwhile became a training establishment for officers of the Fleet Air Arm and an overflow for the Royal Navy barracks. A signal school was also established. A torpedo training section was opened on 22 July 1940.

14. HMS *Titania*

HMS *Titania* was originally built as a merchant ship of 5250 tons (initially intended for the Austrians) and launched March 1915 at the Clyde Shipbuilding Company's yard, Glasgow. She was requisitioned by the Admiralty and commissioned in November 1915 as a submarine depot ship, based at Blyth, with a complement of 249 men under their Commanding Officer, Commander Max K Horton. In Oct 1919, *Titania* was commissioned at Chatham as depot ship for the 4th S/M Flotilla, China, being re-commissioned at Hong Kong 1921, 1924 and 1926. In 1930 she was commissioned at Chatham for the 6th Flotilla based at Weymouth/Portland and in 1935 temporarily with the 3rd Flotilla, Atlantic Fleet. 1935 saw *Titania* as Flagship of the Rear Admiral (Submarines) at the Silver Jubilee Review at Spithead. In 1936 she was attached to 6th Flotilla, Portland. At the 1937 Coronation Review, Spithead, she served as Rear Admiral (Submarines) Flagship, and in1939, was based at Blyth with the 6th Flotilla. In 1940, *Titania* refitted on the Tyne, subsequently serving as Depot Ship for the 10th S/M Flotilla mainly in Holy Loch, for remainder of the war. The exception was her move to serve in Loch Cairnbawn, a sea inlet off Eddrachillis Bay on the west coast of the Scottish Highlands north of Ullapool, a most isolated spot. Known as Port HHZ, it was the site of training for charioteers, Welman one-man submarines and X-Craft four-man midget submarines. In 1945 she was transferred to Portsmouth as depot hulk for the 5th Flotilla until June 1948 when she was broken up at Faslane.

15. Hitler's Commando Order.

On 18th October 1942, after much deliberation by High Command lawyers, officers and staff, Hitler issued his *Kommandobefeh*l or Commando Order in secret, with only 12 copies. The following day Jodl distributed 22 copies with an appendix stating that the order was 'intended for commanders only and must not under any circumstances fall into enemy hands.' The order stated:-

For a long time now our opponents have been employing in their conduct of the war, methods which contravene the International Convention of Geneva. The members of so-called Commandos behave in a particularly brutal and underhand manner; and it has been established that those units recruit criminals not only from their own country but even convicts set free in enemy territories. From captured orders it emerges that they are instructed not only to tie up prisoners, but to kill out-of-hand unarmed captives who they think might prove an encumbrance to them, or hinder them in successfully carrying out their aims. Orders have indeed been found in which the killing of prisoners has positively been demanded of them.

In this connection it has already been notified in an Appendix to Army Orders of 7.10.1942 that in future Germany will adopt the same methods against these Sabotage units of the British and their Allies; i.e. whenever they appear they shall be ruthlessly destroyed by the German troops.

I order, therefore:- from now on all men operating against German troops in so-called Commando raids in Europe or in Africa, are to be annihilated to the last man. This is to be carried out whether they be soldiers in uniform, or saboteurs, with or without arms; and whether fighting or seeking to escape; and it is equally immaterial whether they come into action from Ships and Aircraft, or whether they land by parachute. Even if these individuals on discovery make obvious their intention of giving themselves up as prisoners, no pardon is on any account to be given. On this matter a report is to be made on each case to Headquarters for the information of Higher Command.

Should individual members of these Commandos, such as agents, saboteurs etc. Fall into the hands of the Armed Forces through any means – as, for example, through the Police in one of the Occupied Territories – they are to be instantly handed over to the SD. To hold them in military custody – for example in P.O.W. Camps etc. – even if only as a temporary measure, is strictly forbidden.

This order does not apply to the treatment of those enemy soldiers who are taken prisoner or give themselves up in open battle, in the course of normal operations, large scale attacks; or in major assault landings or airborne operations. Neither does it apply to those who fall into our hands after a sea fight, nor to those enemy soldiers who, after air battle, seek to save their lives by parachute.

I will hold all Commanders and Officers responsible under Military Law for any omission to carry out this order, whether by failure in their duty to instruct their units accordingly, or if they themselves act contrary to it.

16. HORTON, Sir Max Kennedy GCB DSO & 2 bars

Born in 1883 into a military family and the son of a wealthy stockbroker, Max Horton entered the Royal Naval College in Dartmouth, Devon, as an officer cadet on September 15, 1898. At the HMS *Britannia* training school there, he became a cadet captain, outstanding sportsman, and middleweight boxing champion. But he had a wild streak, chafing at authority, being insubordinate, and causing trouble in the mess. His commanding officer's report in October 1907 cited Horton's intelligence and "excellent" leadership qualities but noted that he used bad language and was a "desperate" motorcycle rider.

Horton chose the newly formed submarine service as a career because it was the least stuffy and hidebound branch of the Navy. It offered command at a young age and some freedom from authority and ceremonial ritual. Working closely and relying on each other's technical and professional competence, officers and men enjoyed a special relationship. A submarine commander at sea or under it was independent, and the lone wolf aspect appealed to Horton.

By the outbreak of World War I early in August 1914, Horton was already a lieutenant commander and in charge of one of the first few British ocean-going submarines, the 800-ton HMS *E-9*. He and a handful of other skippers soon distinguished themselves in action despite the fact that the diesel-powered British submarines, unlike U-boats, were plagued by constant mechanical troubles and a shortage of spare parts. On September 13, the *E-9* penetrated the Heligoland Bight and sank the aging German light cruiser *Hela* with two torpedoes from a range of about 600 yards. In celebration, Horton flew a 'Jolly Roger' flag in yellow and black. A few days later, the *E-9* sank the German destroyer *S-116* in enemy waters, celebrating again with a 'Jolly Roger,' this one in black and white, and, by doing so, establishing a tradition in the Royal Navy's submarine service.

While patrolling off the Ems River in north-western Germany on 6th October, 1914, the *E-9* torpedoed and sank the enemy destroyer *S-126*. Horton was awarded the Distinguished Service Order and recommended for early promotion. In December 1914, the *E-9* and two other British submarines were deployed to the frigid Baltic Sea, where they wreaked havoc on German shipping. Horton sank a number of vessels there, including a destroyer, four merchantmen, and a collier, and seriously damaged the cruiser *Prinz Adalbert*. Because of his bold actions, the enemy called the area "Horton's Sea" and put a price on his head.

Horton operated in the North Sea from January 1916 onward and emerged from the First World War as the British submarine commander most feared by the Germans. It was little wonder that during this conflict he was given command of the Baltic Submarine Flotilla. A Russian request for him to be appointed Senior Naval Officer in the Baltic was opposed by the Second Sea Lord, who said, "I understand Commander Horton is something of a pirate and not at all fitted for the position of SNO in the Baltic." The reference to 'pirate' is obvious from Horton's propensity to fly the 'Jolly Roger.' Nevertheless, the audacious submariner was awarded a bar to his DSO and promotion to captain in June 1920 at the age of 37.

After commanding the light cruiser HMS *Conquest* and the 29,150-ton battleship *Resolution* during the 1920s, Horton was promoted to rear admiral in October 1932. He flew his flag aboard the 30,600-ton *Queen Elizabeth*-class battleship *Malaya* for three years and then led the First Cruiser Squadron, flying his flag aboard the 9,830-ton HMS *London*. Given the rank of vice admiral in 1937, he then commanded the Reserve Fleet. He was credited with mobilizing the fleet by the time war came.

At the outbreak of the Second World War, Admiral Horton was placed in command of the Royal Navy's Northern Patrol, which enforced the distant maritime blockade of Germany in the waters between Orkney, Shetland, and the Faeroes. When the Admiralty decided to revitalize the submarine service, Horton was called to take charge in January 1940. Drawing on his First World War experiences, he displayed strategic intuition, achieved a close relationship with Coastal Command when at Western Approaches, and was a tireless leader. Horton was promoted from Captain to Rear Admiral on 17th October 1932, Vice Admiral on 19th August 1936 and Admiral on 9th January 1941. At his own request, to facilitate the promotion of younger officers, he was placed on the Retired List on 16th October 1945.

Admiral Sir Max Kenney Horton died on 30th July 1951 and was accorded the exceptional honour of a State Funeral, celebrated, fittingly, at Liverpool Cathedral. The following words from the poem, 'Christian Ethiks,' written by Thomas Traherne, were printed on the front of the Order of Service:

Strange is the vigour in a brave man's soul.
The strength of his spirit and his irresistible power,
The greatness of his heart and the height of his condition,
His mighty confidence and contempt of dangers,
His true security and repose in himself,
His liberty to dare and do what he pleaseth,
His alacrity in the midst of fears, his invincible temper,
Are advantages which make him master of fortune.
His courage fits him for all attempts,
Makes him serviceable to God and man.
And makes him the bulwark and defence
Of his being and his country.

17. HOWARTH, David Armine, Lieutenant RNVR (1912 – 1990)

Described as a gentle, shy and modest man, Howarth was educated at Tonbridge School, Kent and went on to Trinity College, Cambridge from where he graduated in physics. He joined the RNVR in 1940 on the lower deck but, on the strength of the fact he had recently read a book on navigation, he was placed in reluctant command of a flotilla of seven small ships. A commission followed, with postings first to Scapa Flow as flag lieutenant to the admiral commanding, and then in the early summer of 1941, to Shetland. Under the aegis of SOE, his work for the remainder of the war was to run the Shetland Bus. With the coming of peace he owned and ran a boatyard in Shetland, the last person to build the fishing boats traditional to those islands. As a hobby he wrote about his war work, 'The Shetland Bus' of 1951 becoming a best-seller. The hobby turned to a full-time occupation, and other books followed – 'We Die Alone,' 'Dawn of D-Day,' 'A Near Run Thing' and 'The Nelson Touch.' Howarth's strong, happy ties with Norway remained life-long and, to his amazement and delight, he was knighted there. At his request his ashes were scattered over the waters of Lunna Voe, Shetland, near Lunna House, the first base of the Shetland Bus operation.

18. JOEL, Solomon Barnarto 'Solly'

"Solomon Barnato Joel purchased the Maiden Erlegh Estate in 1903. From his humble start in life, in 1865, as the son of a poor publican, brought up in the tough East End of London, to millionaire diamond dealer is a story in itself. 'Solly' Joel had many business interests including diamond and gold mining, brewing, the City & South London Railway and the Drury Lane Theatre in London. He invested heavily in his Estate, commissioning a wonderful marble swimming pool complete with fresco of nude figures. The grounds were well laid out, featuring a magnificent rose garden and terracing. The Estate also boasted an aviary, polo ground, a cricket field and tennis courts. Joel also established a famous race horse stud at New Farm, which was re-named Home Stud Farm.

After the death of Joel in 1931, the luxurious contents of the mansion were sold at auction, the mansion itself became Maiden Erlegh School for Boys. The school flourished until 1942. In 1945 the building was sold to the Church Army, who used it as a Training College until 1952. ICI then bought the Manor and used it as a conference centre and offices until 1954, when Cooper Estates Ltd purchased the site. Hungarian refugees were housed there, following the Soviet invasion of their country in 1956. They were its last residents – the bulldozers starting their destruction in March 1960. The Stud Farm was purchased in 1932 and continued in existence until the 1980s. The horses were grazed on what is now known as "Laurel Park." From 'A History of Earley' by Ray Harrington-Vail, Earley Town Council, 1988. As late as March, 2022, local residents were able to mount a successful campaign to save Laurel Park from development into a 3G (artificial grass surface) football pitch.

19. The Kharkov Trial

The Kharkov Trial was a war crimes trial held before a Soviet military tribunal in December 1943 in Kharkov, the second largest city of the Ukraine which was at that time part of the Soviet Union. Defendants included one Soviet collaborator, as well as German military, police, and SS personnel responsible for implementing the occupational policies during the German– Soviet War of 1941–45. The trial was the first time that German personnel had been tried for war crimes by the Allies during and after the Second World War.

Units of the German Wehrmacht first occupied Kharkov on 23–24 October 1941. German forces, including the Einsatzgruppen (mobile death squads), killed tens of thousands of Jews, as well as Communists, Soviet prisoners of war, and other "undesirables". Shooting, hanging, and gas vans were used. Fifteen thousand Jews were murdered on 15 December 1941 in a mass shooting in Drobytsky Yar. The Gestapo also shot 435 patients, many of whom were elderly people and children, who were being treated at the local hospital. In March 1943, 800 wounded Red Army soldiers were shot and burned alive. Overall, the Soviets said that in the Kharkov region, the "German-fascist invaders had shot, hanged, burned alive, and poisoned by carbon monoxide gas more than 30,000 peaceful completely innocent citizens, including women, old people, and children."

The city was temporarily retaken by the Red Army in February 1943 and then again by the Wehrmacht in April 1943. Already in the spring of 1943 Soviet authorities discovered mass graves of the victims, mostly Jews. By the time that Kharkov was liberated for good in August 1943, virtually no Jews survived in the city.

The tribunal heard the case against four defendants, Soviet collaborator, Mikhail Bulanov, 26, and three Germans, Wilhelm Langheld, 52, Reinhard Retzlaff, 36, and Hans Ritz, 24, members of the Wehrmacht, police, and SS forces, respectively. They were charged both under the Soviet and international law, the Moscow Declarations. Langheld, Retzlaff, and Ritz were accused in participating in the murders of Soviet citizens, while Bulanov was charged with treason. Prosecutors, defence counsel, and judges were military. A six-person forensic team provided expert testimony and a report concluding that the manner of killings was consistent with shootings and the use of gas.

All four men pleaded guilty, admitting to the crimes and describing them in detail, including the use of the gas vans, mass shootings, and murder of women and children, encouraged and rewarded by their superiors. Langheld admitted to personally killing approximately 100 Soviet citizens. Defence counsel's strategy amounted to arguing that the accused were following orders. The prosecution acknowledged that the men were indeed acting on superior orders, but rejected this as a sufficient defence, using the decision of the Leipzig War Crimes Trials as a precedent. The trial concluded on 18 December 1943 with guilty verdicts and death sentences.

20. LARSEN, Leif Andreas CGM DSO DSC DSM & bar.

As described by Lt Commander David Howarth RNVR, second in command of the base in Shetland from where the fishing boat, *Arthur*, with Larsen in command, set off on Operation TITLE.

'When we invited the crews to elect their own skippers they seldom made a mistake. Leif Larsen was the first to be elected by the vote of the men who had sailed with him, and he turned out to be the finest leader of them all. He did not look the part. He was a stockily built man in his thirties, with china-blue eyes, a broken nose, and a wide humorous mouth; and he had so quiet and modest a manner that it might have taken us a long time to find out his latent powers. But after he became skipper of *Arthur* he soon showed astonishing qualities of a rough and ready leadership and perfectly unshakable courage, and a combination of confidence, bravado and luck which brought him through one adventure after another that would have broken the nerve of most men. By the end of the war he had become the subject of legendary stories in Norway, and the object of devotion among the crews, affection and admiration among his British colleagues, and a certain natural jealousy and mistrust among officers of the Norwegian Navy; all of which left him unmoved, unchanged and unspoilt. He was not only an outstanding figure of our little unit, but one of the most remarkable characters of the war. For his work in our unit he was awarded the Conspicuous Gallantry Medal, the Distinguished Service Medal, and Bar, the Distinguished Service Cross and the Distinguished Service Order, besides, of course, Norwegian decorations. No other man, either British or foreign, has ever received all these British military honours; and this succession of awards was in fact the highest expression of regard which the British Crown could offer. I think the most notable quality of Larsen's character was its stability. He was always the same. His men said he remained the same in battle, equally unruffled. Ultimately we had to make Larsen a sub-lieutenant – not because he cared but so we could give him ciphers which were only issued to officers. The Norwegian Navy were not very willing that he should be promoted and he, for his part, absolutely refused to go to one of their officer training schools. After exhausting all other arguments they discovered he was colour-blind; but in the end common sense won, and Larsen, without training and still remaining his unalterable self, became the most un-officer-like and the most successful sub-lieutenant one could imagine.'

21. MITCHELL, Leslie H, Major, British Army

On meeting Major Mitchell for the first time in 1941, Lt. Howarth described him as 'a thin young man in an army officer's uniform, with a slight forward stoop and anxious expression of short-sightedness. In wartime some people are obscured by their uniform, so that on seeing them one thinks, there is a major or an airman; but others continue to appear as individuals and one says, that is a pleasant or intelligent-looking fellow, and only later notices his rank and service. Mitchell was the latter kind. He was always himself and never primarily a major. He had a wise, kindly face, which did not accord well with the brass buttons, and he had too much sense of the ridiculous and of his own fallibility to be a good parade-ground officer. But he had in plenty the much more valuable qualities of sympathy and humour, and freedom from prejudice and pride. He had an encyclopaedic knowledge of Norwegian politics and psychology. He had been in Oslo when the Germans had arrived and had followed the whole of the campaign. He had seen the initial Norwegian complacency, which decades of neutrality had induced, replaced by an intense national emotion, a strong positive loyalty to their king, a conscious love of their country and a hatred of the Germans which far exceeded the feelings of most Englishmen.'

22. ØEN, Bjarne, Lt. Colonel (1898 – 1994)

Øen was a Norwegian pilot, military officer and Lieutenant General in the Royal Norwegian Air Force. During WWII he played a central role in building up the Royal Norwegian Air

Force in Canada and the United Kingdom. He served as Chief of Defence of Norway from 1957 to 1963. After the occupation of Norway in 1940, he was appointed temporary chief (General Inspector) of the Norwegian Army Air Force. When the NAA Service training camp in southern Ontario (known as Little Norway) was opened in November 1940, Øen was appointed to oversee training. In 1941 he was transferred to London as chief of staff to CinC H Riiser-Larsen.

23. Oslo Western Civil Cemetery

There are no Commonwealth war cemeteries as such in Norway, those who died there being buried in civil cemeteries and churchyards. There is, however, a plot within Oslo Western Civil Cemetery [see Notes 23] which is dedicated to Allied servicemen who died in Norway. Many of the graves there are of airmen shot down while attacking Oslo airport at Fornebu, others being of men killed in crashes during the airborne landings at Oslo, 43 being killed on Liberation Day, 10th May 1945.

In total, the war graves plot at Oslo Western Civil Cemetery contains one hundred and one Commonwealth burials. A Cross of Sacrifice was unveiled in November 1949 by General Otto Ruge, who, at the time of the German invasion was in command of the Norwegian Army. Opposite the Cross is a memorial erected by the City of Oslo in honour of the men of the Commonwealth forces who died in Norway during WWII. Unveiled by HM King Olav of Norway in June 1960, the memorial is in the form of a mourning woman.

24. SAELEN, Frithjof (1917 – 2004)

Born in Bergen, Norway and after schooling, trained there as a writer and illustrator. Upon the German invasion of Norway, Saelen volunteered and fought for his country in the ensuing battles, seeing fighting at Hallingdal. After the capitulation of the regular Norwegian forces, he joined the Norwegian resistance movement as a member of Milorg. Later he became the leader of Milorg's Bergen District until 26 February 1944 when he left Norway, travelling to the UK with Leif Larsen. There he worked for the Norwegian High Command, for which he was awarded the Defence Medal. He wrote a biography of Leif Larsen in 1947, 'Shetlands-Larsen,' translated from Norwegian by Kate Austin Lund. The book was published in the United Kingdom under the title 'None but the Brave,' by Souvenir Press Ltd in 1955, followed by a Corgi edition on 1956. The book sold well and served to a large extent as the source for the 1954 film – Shetlandsgjengen (translated as The Shetland Gang and released as 'Suicide Mission' in the United States) in which Leif Larsen, and several others of the original Shetland Gang, played themselves.

25. SLADEN, Geoffrey Mainwaring 'Slash' DSO & bar DSC MiD CdeG

Sladen was born on 3rd August 1904 in the Reigate district of Surrey and was educated at the Royal Navy colleges at Osborne and Dartmouth before his first sea-going appointment as midshipman in the cruiser, HMS *Hawkins* on the China station in 1922. After a promotion course (HMS Victory, Portsmouth) and a submarine course (HMS *Dolphin*, Portsmouth) Sladen, by now, Sub-Lieutenant, served in HM Submarines L14 and L4. His promotion to Lieutenant in 1927 was followed by appointment as First Lieutenant, HM Submarine L54 then Commanding Officer of HM Submarines H50, *Shark* and *Thames*, *Oswald* and *Trident*. For actions in *Trident* between April 1940 and March 1942, Sladen was awarded the DSO and bar, and the DSC.

It was in 1941 that *Trident* stopped in the Soviet Union for repairs during which time her Captain, Commander Sladen was invited to dine with a Russian admiral. Over dinner Sladen commented to the admiral that his wife was having difficulty pushing her pram through the winter snow back in England. The Russian admiral gave his opinion that what Sladen's wife needed was a reindeer. Sladen gave no more thought to the matter until *Trident* was about to sail, when a reindeer was delivered to the submarine as a present from the admiral, together with a barrel of moss. It was with some difficulty that the animal, given the name Pollyanna by the crew, was brought aboard the submarine via the torpedo loading tube. The name probably derived from Polyarny, Murmansk, which was then adapted by the crew to Pollyanna, the eponymous 11 year old, unfailingly optimistic orphan girl of the book by Eleanor H Porter.

Pollyanna was allocated a berth in the torpedo store area but chose instead to sleep under the Captain's bed. As the six week voyage progressed, and having exhausted her supply of moss, Pollyanna took to eating food scraps from the officer's mess, Carnation condensed milk and the occasional navigation chart. The diet caused Pollyanna to put on weight to the extent

that, when Trident arrived at Blyth, the reindeer was too fat
to disembark via the same means as she had used to come on
board six weeks previously. With great difficulty Pollyanna
was winched up through a hatch and, once on dry land, was
presented to Regent's Park (later London) Zoo where she became
a firm favourite with the keepers and visitors alike. Pollyanna
died at London Zoo in 1947, coincidentally the year that *Trident*
was decommissioned and scrapped.

Commander Sladen, who by June, 1942 was Commanding
Officer of the submarine shore base, HMS *Dolphin*, was
appointed by Admiral Sir Max Horton to develop the specialist
diving suits ('Clammy Deaths') and breathing apparatus (DSEA)
which was to be put to use in Operation Title and subsequent
similar missions. Commanding Officer appointments in the
cruiser HMS *Sheffield*, destroyer *Musketeer* and *Matchless*
were followed by promotion to Captain then, latterly Deputy
Director of Tactical and Staff Duties Division, Admiralty (HMS
President) and finally Senior Officer, Reserve Fleet Portsmouth
and retirement in July 1955. The tobacco firm of W D & H O
Wills issued a series of 50 cigarette cards featuring international
rugby players, No 6 of which featured a caricature of G M
Sladen, United Services, Royal Navy, Hampshire and England.
The reverse reads, "Lieut. Sladen, RN is a typically hard, breezy
sailor-man footballer. Owing to service at sea it was not until the
season 1928-9 that he received his cap and played at the age of
twenty-four, as left centre threequarter against Wales, Ireland
and Scotland. He developed his play in 1925 under the coaching
of the famous scrum-half, C A Kershaw, while at the Royal Naval
College, Greenwich, and was first chosen to play for the Royal

Navy in 1927. Nearly 6 ft in height, he is a hefty attacking player, and in defence, a hard tackler and good touch finder." Captain Sladen died on 4th October, 1985 in the Thornhill district of Dumfriesshire, Scotland.

26. Telavåg Reprisal

On 26th April 1942, after having discovered that some of the inhabitants of Telavåg, a small fishing village 39 km south west of Bergen, were hiding two men of the Norwegian Resistance (Linge Company) the Gestapo arrived to make arrests. Shots were exchanged and two prominent Gestapo officers were killed. The German Reichskommisar, Josef Terboven*, personally oversaw the reprisals which were as quick as they were brutal. As the villagers were made to watch on, all buildings of the village were set on fire and destroyed, all the fishing boats were sunk or confiscated and all the domestic livestock taken away. Many of the men of Telavåg were summarily executed: seventy two were sent to the concentration camp at Sachsenhausen where thirty one were later murdered. The women and children of the village were held in prison for two years. As a further reprisal, eighteen Norwegian prisoners held elsewhere were also executed.

*See – Called to Account.

27. Victoria Terasse, Oslo.

Taken over by the Sicherheitspolize and Sicherheitsdienst in 1940, Victoria Terasse served as their headquarters during the Nazi occupation of Norway. The offices held the interrogation centre for all prisoners in Olso, and the place became synonymous with torture and abuse. On several occasions prisoners jumped out of windows to their death while waiting to be interrogated. Allied bombers tried to destroy the building on 25th September 1942 and on 31st December 1944. They missed on both occasions, sadly instead hitting civilian buildings.

28. WILSON, John Skinner 'Belge,' Lt. Colonel (1888 – 1969)

One-time Head of the World Organisation of the Scout Movement, Wilson was head of the Scandinavian branch of Special Operations Executive during WWII. He was also involved in the Anglo-Norwegian Collaboration Committee for which work he was proclaimed Commander of the Royal Norwegian Order of St Olaf.

Postscript

On 1 June 2022, two French brothers set out to cross Norway on foot from south to north, a journey of 1,720 miles. Using only map and compass for directions, their journey took eighty-three days. Taking the most direct route possible – across marshes, mountains, swamps, heathlands and glaciers – the brothers spent half their time off beaten tracks, fording swollen rivers and passing through snowy terrain. One brother is a mountain and ski guide who teaches orienteering, the other a cartographer. Both regularly compete internationally in orienteering competitions. They received new supplies every few days from their sister and her partner, who drove a safety vehicle along the closest roads. Afterwards, the brothers said they had enjoyed the wild beauty of Norway.

In his grave, Leif Larsen would have given a wry smile.

Timeline

19 December 1941 – Attack on British ships in Alexandria harbour by Italian Navy frogmen

25 February 1942 – German battleship *Tirpitz* commissioned

27 June 1942 – Arctic Convoy PQ17 sails for Russia

3 October 1942 – Operation Basalt Commando raid on Sark

18 October 1942 – Hitler issues his infamous secret Commando Order

26 October 1942 – Operation Title sails from Shetland for Norway

31 October 1942 – Chariots lost from *Arthur* in Trondheimsfjord

7 November 1942 – AB Robert Paul Evans wounded and taken prisoner by the Germans

19 November 1942 – Operation Freshman – gliders take off

21 November 1942 – Survivors of Operation Freshman arrive at Grini Prison

8 December 1942 – Parents of AB Evans learn he is posted as missing

14 December 1942 – AB Evans arrives at Grini Prison

14 January 1943 – AB Evans' 21st birthday

19 January 1943 – AB Evans and five sappers executed by firing squad

12 November 1944 – *Tirpitz* sunk by Nos 9 and 617 Squadrons RAF

?? May 1945 – Mass graves discovered in Trandum Forest

5 September 1945 – Admiralty letter to Mr Evans advising of his son's death

6 October 1946 – Jodl and Keitel, guilty of war crimes, executed by hanging at Nuremburg

10 October 1954 – Norwegians unveil memorial in Trandum Forest

5 May 2020 – Trandum Memorial declared a Norwegian National Cultural Heritage Site.

Author's Acknowledgements

It is with grateful thanks that I acknowledge the large part played in the writing of this book by those who have given me their kind permission to reproduce their own work or that of others, whether held under copyright or not, and the many who have generously and gratuitously contributed images and information from their own collections and recollections. Should it transpire that, despite my best efforts, copyright has not been sought or obtained, or acknowledgement not been duly given where required, the fault lies entirely with me (other than where no reply to my enquiries or requests has been received) and I offer my sincere apologies now with the promise that, upon being informed, I shall ensure the situation is rectified to the best of my ability at the earliest opportunity.

First and foremost, I thank my wife, **Ruth**, for her unfailing support during the writing process. Then, in alphabetical order, **Anabelle**, Archive Curator for the Rights Team, National Museum of the Royal Navy; **Michael Beckett** for information and images relating to Donald Craig; **Patrick Bishop** for kind permission to use information from his book *Target Tirpitz*; **Sophie Bridges**, Archivist, Churchill College, Cambridge, for advice on the Commander Fell papers; **John Callcut**, Seven Seas Club (1922) Ltd, for assistance in research on the ancestry of R.P. Evans; **Magne K Christiansen**, Extra Frosta Coop, for help with Norwegian place names; **Ingrid Christophersen** MBE, of The Anglo–Norse Society, London, for clarification on Norwegian place names; **Clive Clarke**, Navy Search, Restore Records Management, Swadlincote, for details of R.P. Evans' service papers; **Dr Dan Ellin**, University of Lincoln, International Bomber Command Centre Digital Archive, for 'Advice to the relative'; **Commander Torill Herland**, chief of Public Affairs, Royal Norwegian Navy; **Robert W. Hobson**, author of *Chariots of War*, for permission to use information from his book; **Alan Insall**, author of *Secret Alliances*, for permission and encouragement to quote from his book; **Ivar Kraglund**, for details of Norway under German occupation; **Eric Lee**, author of *Operation Basalt*, for generous permission to quote from his book; **Frode Lindgjerdet**, Rustkammeret Armed Forces Museum, Trondheim, and author of *Operasjon Title*, for professional research assistance; **Robert Lyman**, author of *The Real X-MEN*, for permission and encouragement to quote from his book; **Terje R. Meisler**, chief operating officer, Trondheim Port Authority, for translation of nautical terms; **Jorunn Sterten Melhus**, for valuable assistance with place names and history; **Angus Menzies**, commodore RN (Ret'd), for inside information on the submarine service and for research on my behalf; **Bill Moore**, Scalloway Museum, for patiently answering my many queries and for writing the excellent supplement, *Scalloway Then and Now*; the staff at the **National Archives**, Kew; **Dr David Parry**, MA, PhD, Perisher Course survivor RN (Ret'd), for sound advice, kind permission to quote from his book *Perisher* and for his excellent Foreword to this book; **Alan Piper**, secretary, The Brixton Society, for his track and trace efforts; **Steve Rogers**, War Graves Photographic Project, for the valuable work he carries out and for the photo of the gravestone of R.P. Evans; **Patrick Scully** and **Jane Scully** (née Evans), for sharing with me the Evans family history; **Alan Slingsby**, *Brixton Blog & Bugle*, for his track and trace efforts that led to my contact with Patrick and Jane Scully; and **Bjørn Terjesen**, Historian, Naval Academy, for assistance, contacts and map.

Bibliography

Bishop, Patrick, *Target Tirpitz* (London: William Collins, 2012)

Chalmers, Rear Admiral W.S., *Max Horton and the Western Approaches* (London: Hodder & Stoughton, 1954)

Hobson, Robert W., *Chariots of War*, with Foreword by HRH The Duke of Edinburgh (Church Stretton: Ulrich Publishing, 2004)

Howarth, David, Lt Commander (RNVR), *The Shetland Bus* (Edinburgh: Thomas Nelson & Sons Limited, 1951)

Insall, Tony, *Secret Alliances – Special Operations and Intelligence, Norway 1940–1945* (London: Biteback Publishing, 2021).

Lee, Eric, *Operation Basalt – The British Raid on Sark* (Stroud: The History Press, 2016)

Lyman, Robert, *The Real X-MEN. The Heroic Story of the Underwater War 1942–1945* (London: Quercus Editions Ltd, 2015)

Saelen, Frithjof, *None But The Brave*, translated from the Norwegian by Kate Austin Lund (England: Souvenir Press Ltd, 1955; Corgi, 1956)

Schofield, Vice Admiral B.B., *The Arctic Convoys* (London: Macdonald and Jane's Publishers Ltd, 1977)

Warren, C.E.T. and Benson, James, *Above Us The Waves – The Story of Midget Submarines and Human Torpedoes* (London: George G. Harrap & Co Ltd, 1953)

Wiggan, Richard, *Operation FRESHMAN – The Rjukan Heavy Water Raid 1942* (London: William Kimber & Co Ltd, 1986)

Woodman, Captain Richard, LVO, *The Real Cruel Sea* (London: John Murray Publishers, 2004)

Files from the National Archives, Kew

WO 311/383: Killing of survivors from Operation Freshman, destruction of heavy water plant in Norway and killing of survivor of attack on German battleship *Tirpitz*, Trondheim, Norway

WO 309/720: Operation Freshman, destruction of heavy water plant in Norway; killing of commandos

WO 331/16: Operation Freshman, destruction of heavy water plant at Rjukan Norway; killing of survivors of raid at Stavanger, Norway

HS 2/202: Operation Title; abortive chariot attack on *Tirpitz*

HS 2/203: Operation Title; abortive chariot attack on *Tirpitz*

ADM 358/2199: Able Seaman R.P Evans: missing; Operation Title, November 1942, reported to have been shot dead, January 1943

FO 950/3010: Nazi persecution claim: Mrs Rose Catherine Evans for Mr Robert Paul Evans (deceased)

Index to Contents

Index to Notes